OLINESS

—ABRIDGED—

J. C. RYLE

HOLINESS

—ABRIDGED—

Its Nature, Hindrances, Difficulties, and Roots

FOREWORD BY JOHN MacARTHUR

MOODY CLASSICS

MOODY PUBLISHERS
CHICAGO

2010 edition by
THE MOODY BIBLE INSTITUTE
OF CHICAGO

All Scripture quotations are taken from the King James Version.

Interior Design: Smartt Guys design
Cover Design: Kirk DouPonce / Dog Eared Design
Photo Credit: Bildarchiv Preussischer Kulturbesitz / Art Resource, NY
        Friedrich, Caspar David (1774-1840)
        Riesengebirge with Rising Fog. Ca. 1819-1820. Oil on canvas, 54.9
        x 70.4 cm. Inv. 8858.
        Location :Neue Pinakothek, Bayerische
        Staatsgemaeldesammlungen, Munich, Germany
Biographical Introduction by Brandon O'Brien

Library of Congress Cataloging-in-Publication Data

Ryle, J. C. (John Charles), 1816-1900.
 Holiness : its nature, hindrances, difficulties, and roots / J. C. Ryle.
    p. cm.
 ISBN 978-0-8024-5455-3
 1. Holiness. I. Title.
 BT767.R95 2010
 234'.8—dc22

                                2010005420

We hope you enjoy this book from Moody Publishers. Our goal is to provide high-quality, thought-provoking books and products that connect truth to your real needs and challenges. For more information on other books and products written and produced from a biblical perspective, go to www.moodypublishers.com or write to:

Moody Publishers
820 N. LaSalle Boulevard
Chicago, IL 60610

7 9 10 8 6

Printed in the United States of America

CONTENTS

Foreword

by John MacArthur

∾

BISHOP J. C. RYLE'S *Holiness* deserves a place near the top of any list of must-read books. Written in a simple, easily accessible style, this is nevertheless one of the finest theological works you will ever read—proving again that doctrine does not need to be treated in a sterile, abstruse, or academic manner in order to be profound. This book is also the most practical and helpful of all the counseling resources I keep in my library.

Ryle wrote *Holiness* to answer some fashionable but dangerous teachings about sanctification, the Christian's struggle with sin, and the so-called deeper life. By the second half of the nineteenth century, conservative evangelicals in Britain and America had begun to develop an unprecedented infatuation with mystical, experiential, inward-looking concepts of personal holiness. The result was widespread confusion regarding the biblical doctrine of sanctification. Ryle was a refreshing voice of biblical clarity in the midst of many muddled and deluded views. This book was his most important and most enduring answer to the Holiness movement, and it is as relevant and helpful today as ever.

What was the source of so much confusion? Several varieties of perfectionist and second-blessing doctrines had been gradually gaining grass-roots popularity in evangelical circles worldwide since the time of John Wesley. A new wave of perfectionist doctrines followed the Second Great Awakening in America, and by mid-century those ideas were already finding eager acceptance in the United Kingdom. Charles Finney, long enamored with perfectionist teachings, visited England twice (1849–51 and 1858–50). Robert Pearsall Smith, a Philadelphia-based perfectionist of Quaker descent, toured England in 1873–75, lecturing on "the higher life." His wife, Hannah Whitall Smith, lectured on that tour as well and wrote most of her famous work *The Christian's Secret of a Happy Life* during those years in England.

The Smiths' message took British evangelicalism by storm. It was a toned-down variety of Wesleyan perfectionism blended with Quaker quietism. Whereas Wesley had taught that believers may achieve entire sanctification through the complete eradication of the old nature and habits, the Smiths said the believer's sin nature remains fully alive and teeming with mischievous potential. Nevertheless, they said, the fleshly old nature can easily be subdued—in effect, completely neutralized—as long as we relinquish control of our bodies, hearts, and minds to Christ.

According to this view, key to victory is passive faith. The believer's only duty is to trust God. All the effort in sanctification is God's; the faithful believer only needs to rest in the Lord. The key words in most deeper-life teaching therefore lay a heavy stress on the passive element: *surrender, yield, trust, rest.* Those are all important biblical expressions, of course—but by no means do they give us the believer's *only* duty in the struggle against sin.

Yet the Smiths' deeper-life teaching emphatically denied that sanctification entails any kind of "struggle." Victory was characterized as life on a higher spiritual plane where temptation would cease to trouble the consecrated person. At one point in her book Mrs. Smith acknowledges that Scripture compares the Christian life to perpetual warfare. She describes it oxymoronically as wrestling against spiritual enemies while we remain seated with Christ in heavenly places. She does not seem to grasp that victory in the warfare also requires us to struggle fiercely against earthly sins and temptation. Indeed, when she addresses the issue of *temptation*, she says the way to meet any enticement to sin is "to hand the temptation over to our Lord, and trust Him to conquer it for us." Expressions such as that have become so common that twenty-first-century evangelicals no longer evaluate them critically. But Scripture never speaks in such terms. When we are faced with real temptation, we are commanded to flee (1 Corinthians 6:18; 10:14; 1 Timothy 6:11; 2 Timothy 2:22). Resisting the devil is just as important as resting in the Lord (James 4:7). But the Smiths' teaching consistently downplayed countless commands like those in Scripture. For them, "victory" was something to be received by faith, not an actual triumph won through strife or conflict.

The same year Mrs. Smith's book was published, the Keswick Convention was founded in England's Lake District to promote a similar view of holiness. (The Convention is named for the town in Cumbria where the organization's annual conference has been held since 1875.)

Like the Smiths' higher-life concept, Keswick doctrine stressed a totally passive approach to sanctification, promising an easy, instant pathway to victory over all known sin. The movement's message was often summed up with the slogan "Let go and let God."

Keswick's founders were an Anglican and a Quaker, and conference speakers were predominantly conservative evangelical Anglicans, including a young scholar named Handley Moule, who later became bishop of Durham. The Keswick movement therefore became the main conduit by which deeper-life teaching came into the circle of J. C. Ryle's influence and ministry, and the impact was both sudden and profound. Evangelical lay people came in large crowds to Keswick, then returned to their parish churches filled with zeal for deeper-life teaching, yet often utterly failing to realize true and lasting victory over sin in the real world. Some adopted antinomian views in order to reconcile their beliefs with their experience. But a number of disillusioned deeper-life aficionados (including Robert Pearsall Smith himself) ultimately abandoned the faith completely.

J. C. Ryle clearly saw the dangers very early, and he addresses them in careful detail in this book. Remarkably, Ryle's
Holiness was first published just two years after the founding of
the Keswick Convention, and no one has yet written a finer
exposé of the dangers of deeper-life teaching.

Bishop Ryle was well situated to respond to the deeper-life
movement. He had been converted at the age of twenty while
hearing Ephesians 2 read in church. That chapter, of course,
stresses the doctrine of justification by faith alone and the truth
that our salvation from start to finish is all God's work: "For by
grace you have been saved through faith; and that not of yourselves, it is the gift of God; not as a result of works, so that no one
may boast. For we are His workmanship" (Ephesians 2:8–10).
That is the very truth most of the deeper-life teachers believed
they were preserving.

But Ephesians 2:10 continues and makes a vital point: "We
are His workmanship, created in Christ Jesus *for good works*,
which God prepared beforehand so that we would walk in them"
(emphasis added). There is work for the believer to do, once we
have been justified (made right with God) by faith alone. There is
a vast difference between justification (which of course is received by faith, totally apart from any works or merit on the sinner's part) and sanctification (which entails good works and
enjoins our efforts in a lifelong travail against sin). By failing to
distinguish properly between justification and sanctification, the
so-called holiness doctrines were actually thwarting true holiness.

Near the end of chapter 2, Ryle includes an extended point-by-point comparison and contrast between justification and sanctification. Don't breeze through that section lightly. It is one of the foundational points on which Ryle builds his case. He outlines a set of distinctions that are supremely helpful in clearing away the kind of confusion that is typically bred by deeper-life teaching.

And yet, this book is not a polemical diatribe against the deeper life doctrines. Throughout, Ryle presents the biblical truth of sanctification in positive terms with careful, thorough, convincing biblical support. The result is a definitive treatise on the doctrine of sanctification that stands solidly on its own in any context.

J. C. Ryle was not generally a writer of book-length studies. Tracts and pamphlet-sized articles were his specialty. His books are all compilations of short articles, tracts, and sermons. (Note how Ryle refers to the chapters as "papers" in the opening sentence of his introduction.) *Holiness* grew from a compilation of four brief tracts Ryle had written on the subjects of sin, sanctification, and assurance. Seeing the need for a more substantial work, Ryle expanded and developed those four tracts, tying them together with new material to form the heart of this book. It was the most ambitious writing project he ever undertook. The first edition was published in 1877, comprising seven chapters. A greatly expanded second edition was published two years later, adding thirteen pamphlets and sermons that illustrate and fortify the biblical case set forth in those seven original chapters. This edition, abridged for a generation accustomed to reading in smaller bites, includes six of the original seven chapters (chapters 1–6, omitting only the chapter on assurance) and three of the supplementary chapters (7–9). The heart and flavor of Ryle's original editions have thus been retained in a format that contemporary readers will find more inviting.

I love Ryle's style for its unusual clarity and unflinching faithfulness to Scripture. He addresses the issue of sin, for example, with refreshing candor; his approach to handling doctrine is expository first, then systematic; and he is always faithful to the text (and context) of whatever Scripture he deals with.

Some fifty years ago, D. Martyn Lloyd-Jones wrote a brief foreword to an edition of Ryle's *Holiness*. Lloyd-Jones succinctly described the book with these words: "Ryle, like his great masters [the Puritans], has no easy way to holiness to offer us, and no 'patent' method by which it can be obtained; but he invariably produces that 'hunger and thirst after righteousness' which is the only indispensable condition to being 'filled.'"

Exactly.

Sadly, the errors unleashed into the evangelical movement by holiness teachers more than a century and a half ago still cause much confusion today. The doctrine of sanctification is still widely misunderstood despite its massive implications for Christian living. That makes the need for this book as great as ever. No doubt the need is actually greater than ever, because we live in a generation that has shown a declining interest in doctrinal understanding, while a multitude of churches are decreasing their emphasis and their dependence on Scripture. Ryle's book offers a helpful antidote to all those issues. I'm extremely grateful to Moody for making it more widely available in this new, streamlined edition. I hope it will be read with fresh interest and its truths passed on to the next generation. And I hope it will whet your appetite for more of Ryle's excellent works.

JOHN MACARTHUR

Biographical Introduction

J. C. (John Charles) Ryle
(1816–1900)

∽

ALMOST FROM HIS BIRTH on May 10, 1816 in Cheshire, England, John Charles Ryle was on a trajectory for greatness. Ryle was born into privilege; his father had inherited a fortune made in the silk trade. Perhaps more importantly, the young Ryle was charming and handsome, physically strong, and mentally sharp.

Ryle loved to play cricket as a child, and during his time at Oxford University, he was captain of the school team. Years later Ryle credited his experience as a cricketer with helping him to develop his remarkable leadership abilities. Nevertheless, he didn't allow cricket to distract him from his studies. He finished his academic training with such distinction that his instructors invited him to stay on at Oxford as a tutor. But Ryle declined; he intended to enter a life of public service. He studied law for a few months before joining his father to work at the family bank.

Ryle's hopes for a career in public service were shattered when his family lost their fortune—quite literally—overnight. Due to the misdealing of a subordinate worker, the Ryle Bank went bankrupt. Just like that, Ryle had lost his inheritance and his chance of entering politics.

If Ryle had always been wealthy, charming, and talented, he was not particularly religious until into adulthood. In 1838, he fell ill and, for the first time in his life, began to take prayer and Scripture reading seriously. Shortly thereafter, he found himself in a church service in which someone was reading from Ephesians 2. He was struck in particular by verse 8: "For by grace are ye saved through faith; and that not of yourselves: it is the gift of God." Then and there he surrendered his whole life to Christ.

In 1841, Ryle was ordained as a minister in the Church of England. In his first position in a rural parish he developed the plain and direct style of communication that would mark his future ministry. He served at several churches for the next forty years, during which time he wrote hundreds of evangelistic tracts. He was a wildly popular writer. His tracts sold more than 12 million copies in his lifetime, and were eventually translated into about a dozen European and Asian languages.

While his ministry flourished, Ryle's home life was challenging. In 1844, he married his first wife, who died in 1847. He married again in 1849. The couple was happy, but his wife's health was poor, so the pastor seldom travelled and practically raised his children alone. When his second wife died in 1860, he became a single father with five children between two and fourteen years old.

Despite these hardships, Ryle became a leader among the

evangelical clergy in his day. In 1880, he was appointed the first bishop of the newly formed diocese of Liverpool. Because the diocese was new, it had no system of leadership, no formal administration. During his tenure as Bishop of Liverpool, Ryle raised enough funds to build ninety new houses of worship, ordained over five hundred deacons, five hundred priests, and at least forty-five salaried lay Scripture readers and thirty-one "Bible women." These were women who were sent into some of the worst of the slums of Liverpool, places men could not go. They not only taught, but they demonstrated their faith by works of mercy and by example. Ryle also founded the Lay Helpers Association, an organization that oversaw Sunday schools, Bible classes, mission services, and cared for the sick.

The promotion to bishop didn't alter Ryle's character. He made it clear from the beginning that he would not engage in partisan politics in his new post. "You know my positions; I am a committed man," he wrote in response to his appointment. "I come among you a Protestant and Evangelical Bishop of the Church of England . . . I come with a desire to hold out the right hand to all loyal Churchmen, by whatever name they are know, holding at the same time my own opinions determinedly." He served as Bishop of Liverpool until he retired on March 1, 1900. He died just a few months later on June 10, 1900.

Written in 1877, Ryle's book *Holiness* is exemplary of his preaching style: direct, clear, and logically compelling. Teaching on holiness was fashionable in Ryle's day, but he felt that much of the popular work on the subject was shallow and misguided. In response Ryle offered *Holiness* as a counter argument for the biblical foundations of sanctification.

Sin

cx

"SIN IS THE TRANSGRESSION OF THE LAW." *(1 John 3:4)*

HE WHO WISHES to attain right views about Christian holiness must begin by examining the vast and solemn subject of sin. He must dig down very low if he would build high. A mistake here is most mischievous. Wrong views about holiness are generally traceable to wrong views about human corruption. I make no apology for beginning this volume about holiness by making some plain statements about *sin*.

The plain truth is that a right knowledge of sin lies at the root of all saving Christianity. Without it such doctrines as justification, conversion, sanctification, are "words and names" that convey no meaning to the mind. The first thing, therefore, that God does when He makes anyone a new creature in Christ is to send light into his heart and show him that he is a guilty sinner. The material creation in Genesis began with "light," and so also does the spiritual creation. God "shines into our hearts" by the work of the Holy Ghost, and then spiritual life begins (2 Cor. 4:6). Dim or indistinct views of sin are the origin of most of the errors, heresies, and false doctrines of the present day. If a man does not realize the dangerous nature of his soul's disease, you cannot wonder if he is content with false or imperfect remedies. I believe that one of the chief wants of the church has been, and is, clearer, fuller teaching about sin.

(1) I shall begin the subject by supplying some definition of sin. We are all of course familiar with the terms "sin" and "sinners." We talk frequently of "sin" being in the world, and of men committing "sins." But what do we mean by these terms and phrases? Do we really know? I fear there is much mental confusion and haziness on this point. Let me try, as briefly as possible, to supply an answer.

I say, then, that "sin," speaking generally, is, as the Ninth Article of our Church [the Church of England] declares, the fault and corruption of the nature of every man who is naturally engendered of the offspring of Adam; whereby man is very far gone [*quam longissime* is the Latin] from original righteousness, and is of his own nature inclined to evil, so that the flesh lusts always against the spirit; and, therefore, in every person born into the world, it deserves God's wrath and damnation.

Sin, in short, is that vast moral disease that affects the whole human race, of every rank, and class, and name, and nation, and people, and tongue; a disease from which there never was but one born of woman who was free. Need I say that One was Christ Jesus the Lord?

I say, furthermore, that "a sin," to speak more particularly, consists in doing, saying, thinking, or imagining, anything that is not in perfect conformity with the mind and law of God. "Sin," in short, as the Scripture says, is "the transgression of the law" (1 John 3:4). The slightest outward or inward departure from absolute mathematical parallelism with God's revealed will and character constitutes a sin, and at once makes us guilty in God's sight.

Of course I need not tell anyone who reads his Bible with attention, that a man may break God's law in heart and thought, when there is no overt and visible act of wickedness. Our Lord has settled that point beyond dispute in the Sermon on the Mount (Matt. 5:21–28). Even a poet of our own has truly said, "A man may smile and smile, and be a villain."

Again, I need not tell a careful student of the New Testament that there are sins of omission as well as commission, and that we sin, as our Prayer Book justly reminds us, by "leaving undone the things we ought to do," as really as by "doing the things we ought not to do." The solemn words of our Master in the Gospel of St. Matthew place this point also beyond dispute. It is there written, "Depart, ye cursed, into everlasting fire"; "for I was an hungered, and ye gave me no meat; I was thirsty, and ye gave me no drink" (Matt. 25:41–42). It was a deep and thoughtful saying of holy Archbishop Ussher, just before he died—"Lord, forgive me all my sins, and specially my sins of omission."

But I do think it necessary in these times to remind my readers that a man may commit sin and yet be ignorant of it, and fancy himself innocent when he is guilty. I fail to see any scriptural warrant for the modern assertion that "Sin is not sin to us until we discern it and are conscious of it." On the contrary, in the fourth and fifth chapters of that unduly neglected book, Leviticus, and in the fifteenth of Numbers, I find Israel distinctly taught that there were sins of ignorance, which rendered people unclean, and needed atonement (Lev. 4:1–35; 5:14–19; Num. 15:25–29). And I find our Lord expressly teaching that "the servant who knew not his master's will and did it not" was not excused on account of his ignorance, but was "beaten" or punished (Luke 12:48). We shall do well to remember that when we make our own miserably imperfect knowledge and consciousness the measure of our sinfulness, we are on very dangerous ground. A deeper study of Leviticus might do us much good.

(2) Concerning the origin and source of this vast moral disease called "sin," I must say something. I fear the views of many professing Christians on this point are sadly defective and unsound. I dare not pass it by. Let us, then, have it fixed down in our minds that the sinfulness of man does not begin from without, but from within. It is not the result of bad training in early years. It is not picked up from bad companions and bad examples, as some weak Christians are too fond of saying. No! it is a family disease, which we all inherit from our first parents, Adam and Eve, and with which we are born. Created "in the image of God,"

innocent and righteous at first, our parents fell from original righteousness and became sinful and corrupt. And from that day to this all men and women are born in the image of fallen Adam and Eve, and inherit a heart and nature inclined to evil. "By one man sin entered into the world." "That which is born of the flesh is flesh." "We are by nature children of wrath." "The carnal mind is enmity against God." "Out of the heart [naturally as out of a fountain] proceed evil thoughts, adulteries," and the like (Rom. 5:12; John 3:6; Eph. 2:3; Rom. 8:7; Mark 7:21). The fairest babe who has entered life this year, and become the sunbeam of a family, is not, as its mother perhaps fondly calls it, a little "angel," or a little "innocent," but a little "sinner." Alas! as it lies smiling and crowing in its cradle, that little creature carries in its heart the seeds of every kind of wickedness! Only watch it carefully, as it grows in stature and its mind develops, and you will soon detect in it an incessant tendency to that which is bad, and a backwardness to that which is good. You will see in it the buds and germs of deceit, evil temper, selfishness, self-will, obstinacy, greediness, envy, jealousy, passion, which, if indulged and let alone, will shoot up with painful rapidity. Who taught the child these things? Where did he learn them? The Bible alone can answer these questions! Of all the foolish things that parents say about their children there is none worse than the common saying, "My son has a good heart at the bottom. He is not what he ought to be; but he has fallen into bad hands. Public schools are bad places. The tutors neglect the boys. Yet he has a good heart at the bottom." The truth, unhappily, is diametrically the other way. The first cause of all sin lies in the natural corruption of the boy's own heart, and not in the school.

(3) Concerning the extent of this vast moral disease of man called sin, let us beware that we make no mistake. The only safe ground is that which is laid for us in Scripture. "Every imagination of the thoughts of his heart" is by nature evil and that "continually." "The heart is deceitful above all things, and desperately wicked" (Gen. 6:5; Jer. 17:9). Sin is a disease that pervades and runs through every part of our moral constitution and every faculty of our minds. The understanding, the affections, the reasoning powers, the will, are all more or less infected. Even the conscience is so blinded that it cannot be depended on as a sure guide, and is as likely to lead men wrong as right, unless it is enlightened by the Holy Ghost. In short, "from the sole of the foot even unto the head there is no soundness" about us (Isa. 1:6). The disease may be veiled under a thin covering of courtesy, politeness, good manners, and outward decorum; but it lies deep down in the constitution.

I admit fully that man has many grand and noble faculties left about him, and that in arts and sciences and literature he shows immense capacity. But the fact still remains that in spiritual things he is utterly "dead," and has no natural knowledge, or love, or fear of God. His best things are so interwoven and intermingled with corruption, that the contrast only brings out into sharper relief the truth and extent of the Fall. That one and the same creature should be in some things so high and in others so low—so great and yet so little—so noble and yet so mean—so grand in his conception and execution of material things, and yet so groveling and debased in his affections—that he should be able to plan and erect buildings like those at Carnac and Luxor in Egypt, and the Parthenon at Athens, and yet worship vile gods and goddesses, and birds, and beasts, and creeping things—that he should be able to produce tragedies like those of Aeschylus and Sophocles, and histories like that of Thucydides, and yet be a slave to abominable vices like those described in the first chapter of the Epistle to the Romans—all this is a sore puzzle to those who sneer at "God's Word written," and scoff at us as bibliolaters. But it is a knot that we can untie with the Bible in our hands. We can acknowledge that man has all the marks of a majestic temple about him—a temple in which God once dwelt, but a temple that is now in utter ruins—a temple in which a shattered window here, and a doorway there, and a column there, still give some faint idea of the magnificence of the original design, but a temple that from end to end has lost its glory and fallen from its high estate. And we say that nothing solves the complicated problem of man's condition but the doctrine of original or birth-sin and the crushing effects of the Fall.

Let us remember, besides this, that every part of the world bears testimony to the fact that sin is the *universal disease of all mankind.* Search the globe from east to west and from pole to pole—search every nation of every clime in the four quarters of the earth—search every rank and class in our own country from the highest to the lowest—and under every circumstance and condition, the report will be always the same. The remotest islands in the Pacific Ocean, completely separate from Europe, Asia, Africa, and America, beyond the reach alike of Oriental luxury and Western arts and literature—islands inhabited by people ignorant of books, money, steam, and gunpowder—uncontaminated by the vices of modern civilization, these very islands have always been found, when first discovered, the abode of the vilest forms of lust, cruelty, deceit, and superstition. If the inhabitants have known nothing else, they have always known how to sin! Everywhere the human heart is naturally "deceitful above all things, and desperately wicked" (Jer. 17:9). For my part, I know no stronger proof of the inspiration of Genesis and the Mosaic account of the origin of man, than the power, extent, and universality of sin. Grant that mankind have all sprung from one pair, and that this pair fell (as Gen. 3 tells us), and the state of human nature everywhere is easily accounted for. Deny it, as many do, and you are at once involved in inexplicable difficulties. In a word, the uniformity and universality of human corruption supply one of the most unanswerable instances of the enormous "difficulties of atheism."

After all, I am convinced that the greatest proof of the extent and power of sin is the pertinacity with which it cleaves to man even after he is converted and has become the subject of the Holy Ghost's operations. To use the language of the Ninth Article, "this infection of nature doth remain—yea, even in them that are regenerate." So deeply planted are the roots of human corruption, that even after we are born again, renewed, "washed, sanctified, justified," and made living members of Christ, these roots remain alive in the bottom of our hearts, and, like the leprosy in the walls of the house, we never get rid of them until the earthly house of this tabernacle is dissolved. Sin, no doubt, in the believer's heart, has no longer dominion. It is checked, controlled, mortified, and crucified by the expulsive power of the new principle of grace. The life of a believer is a life of victory and not of failure. But the very struggles that go on within his bosom, the fight that he finds it needful to fight daily, the watchful jealousy that he is obliged to exercise over his inner man, the contest between the flesh and the spirit, the inward "groanings" that no one knows but he who has experienced them—all, all testify to the same great truth, all show the enormous power and vitality of sin. Mighty indeed must that foe be who even when crucified is still alive! Happy is that believer who understands it, and while he rejoices in Christ Jesus has no confidence in the flesh; and while he says, "Thanks be unto God who giveth us the victory," never forgets to watch and pray lest he fall into temptation!

(4) Concerning the guilt, vileness, and offensiveness of sin in the sight of God, my words shall be few. I say "few" advisedly. I do not think, in the nature of things, that mortal man can at all realize the exceeding sinfulness of sin in the sight of that holy and perfect One with whom we have to do. On the one hand, God

is that eternal Being who "chargeth his angels with folly," and in whose sight the very "heavens are not clean." He is One who reads thoughts and motives as well as actions, and requires "truth in the inward parts" (Job 4:18; 15:15; Ps. 51:6). We, on the other hand—poor blind creatures, here today and gone tomorrow, born in sin, surrounded by sinners, living in a constant atmosphere of weakness, infirmity, and imperfection—can form none but the most inadequate conceptions of the hideousness of evil. We have no line to fathom it, and no measure by which to gauge it. The blind man can see no difference between a masterpiece of Titian or Raphael and the Queen's head on a village signboard. The deaf man cannot distinguish between a penny whistle and a cathedral organ. The very animals whose smell is most offensive to us have no idea that they are offensive, and are not offensive to one another. And man, fallen man, I believe, can have no just idea what a vile thing sin is in the sight of that God whose handiwork is absolutely perfect—perfect whether we look through telescope or microscope—perfect in the formation of a mighty planet like Jupiter, with his satellites, keeping time to a second as he rolls round the sun—perfect in the formation of the smallest insect that crawls over a foot of ground. But let us nevertheless settle it firmly in our minds that sin is "the abominable thing that God hates"— that God "is of purer eyes than to behold iniquity, and cannot look upon that which is evil"—that the least transgression of God's law makes us "guilty of all"—that "the soul that sinneth shall die"—that "the wages of sin is death"—

that God shall "judge the secrets of men"—that there is a worm that never dies, and a fire that is not quenched that "the wicked shall be turned into hell" and "shall go away into everlasting punishment"—and that "nothing that defiles shall in any wise enter heaven" (Jer. 44:4; Hab. 1:13; James 2:10; Ezek. 18:4; Rom. 6:23; 2:16; Mark 9:44; Ps. 9:17; Matt. 25:46; Rev. 21:27). These are indeed tremendous words, when we consider that they are written in the book of a most merciful God!

No proof of the fullness of sin, after all, is so overwhelming and unanswerable as the cross and passion of our Lord Jesus Christ, and the whole doctrine of His substitution and atonement. Terribly black must that guilt be for which nothing but the blood of the Son of God could make satisfaction. Heavy must that weight of human sin be that made Jesus groan and sweat drops of blood in agony at Gethsemane, and cry at Golgotha, "My God, my God, why hast thou forsaken me?" (Matt. 27:46). Nothing, I am convinced, will astonish us so much, when we awake in the resurrection day, as the view we shall have of sin, and the retrospect we shall take of our own countless shortcomings and defects. Never till the hour when Christ comes the second time shall we fully realize the "sinfulness of sin." Well might George Whitefield say, "The anthem in heaven will be, What hath God wrought!"

(5) One point only remains to be considered on the subject of sin, which I dare not pass over. That point is its deceitfulness. It is a point of most serious importance, and I venture to think it

does not receive the attention that it deserves. You may see this deceitfulness in the wonderful proneness of men to regard sin as less sinful and dangerous than it is in the sight of God; and in their readiness to extenuate it, make excuses for it, and minimize its guilt. "It is but a little one! God is merciful! God is not extreme to mark what is done amiss! We mean well! One cannot be so particular! Where is the mighty harm? We only do as others!" Who is not familiar with this kind of language? You may see it in the long string of smooth words and phrases that men have coined in order to designate things that God calls downright wicked and ruinous to the soul. What do such expressions as "fast," "gay," "wild," "unsteady," "thoughtless," "loose" mean? They show that men try to cheat themselves into the belief that sin is not quite so sinful as God says it is, and that they are not so bad as they really are. You may see it in the tendency even of believers to indulge their children in questionable practices, and to blind their own eyes to the inevitable result of the love of money, of tampering with temptation, and sanctioning a low standard of family religion. I fear we do not sufficiently realize the extreme subtlety of our soul's disease. We are too apt to forget that temptation to sin will rarely present itself to us in its true colors, saying, "I am your deadly enemy, and I want to ruin you forever in hell." Oh no! sin comes to us, like Judas, with a kiss; and like Joab, with an outstretched hand and flattering words. The forbidden fruit seemed good and desirable to Eve; yet it cast her out of Eden. The walking idly on his palace roof seemed harmless enough to David; yet it ended in adultery and murder. Sin rarely seems sin at first beginnings. Let us then watch and pray, lest we fall into temptation. We may give wickedness smooth names, but we cannot alter its nature and character in the sight of God. Let us remember St. Paul's words: "Exhort one another daily, lest any be hardened through the deceitfulness of sin" (Heb. 3:13). It is a wise prayer in our Litany, "From the deceits of the world, the flesh, and the devil, good Lord, deliver us."

And now, before I go further, let me briefly mention two thoughts that appear to me to rise with irresistible force out of the subject.

On the one hand, I ask my readers to observe what deep reasons we all have for *humiliation and self-abasement*. Let us sit down before the picture of sin displayed to us in the Bible, and consider what guilty, vile, corrupt creatures we all are in the sight of God. What need we all have of that entire change of heart called regeneration, new birth, or conversion! What a mass of infirmity and imperfection cleaves to the very best of us at our very best! What a solemn thought it is, that "without holiness no man shall see the Lord" (Heb. 12:14)! What cause we have to cry with the publican, every night in our lives, when we think of our sins of omission as well as commission, "God be merciful to me a sinner!" (Luke 18:13). How admirably suited are the general and Communion Confessions of the Prayer Book to the actual condition of all professing Christians! How well that language suits

God's children, which the Prayer Book puts in the mouth of every churchman before he goes up to the Communion Table: "The remembrance of our misdoings is grievous unto us; the burden is intolerable. Have mercy upon us, have mercy upon us, most merciful Father; for thy Son our Lord Jesus Christ's sake, forgive us all that is past." How true it is that the holiest saint is in himself a miserable sinner, and a debtor to mercy and grace to the last moment of his existence!

With my whole heart I subscribe to that passage in Hooker's sermon on justification, which begins,

> Let the holiest and best things we do be considered. We are never better affected unto God than when we pray; yet when we pray, how are our affections many times distracted! How little reverence do we show unto the grand majesty of God unto whom we speak! How little remorse of our own miseries! How little taste of the sweet influence of his tender mercies do we feel! Are we not as unwilling many times to begin, and as glad to make an end, as if in saying, "Call upon me," he had set us a very burdensome task? It may seem somewhat extreme, which I will speak; therefore, let every one judge of it, even as his own heart shall tell him, and not otherwise; I will but only make a demand! If God should yield unto us, not as unto Abraham—if fifty, forty, thirty, twenty—yea, or if ten good persons could be found in a city, for their sakes this city should not be destroyed; but,

and if he should make us an offer thus large, "search all the generations of men since the fall of our father Adam, find one man that hath done one action which hath passed from him pure, without any stain or blemish at all; and for that one man's only action neither man nor angel should feel the torments which are prepared for both," do you think that this ransom to deliver men and angels could be found to be among the sons of men? The best things which we do have somewhat in them to be pardoned.[1]

That witness is true. For my part I am persuaded the more light we have, the more we see our own sinfulness: the nearer we get to heaven, the more we are clothed with humility. In every age of the church you will find it true, if you will study biographies, that the most eminent saints—men like Bradford, Rutherford, and McCheyne—have always been the humblest men.

On the other hand, I ask my readers to observe *how deeply thankful we ought to be for the glorious gospel of the grace of God.* There is a remedy revealed for man's need, as wide and broad and deep as man's disease. We need not be afraid to look at sin, and study its nature, origin, power, extent, and vileness, if we only look at the same time at the almighty medicine provided for us in the salvation that is in Jesus Christ. Though sin has abounded, grace has much more abounded. Yes: in the everlasting covenant of redemption, to which Father, Son, and Holy Ghost are parties —in the Mediator of that covenant, Jesus Christ the righteous, perfect God and perfect Man in one Person—in the work that He did by dying for our sins and rising again for our justification—in the offices that He fills as our Priest, Substitute, Physician, Shepherd, and Advocate—in the precious blood He shed, which can cleanse from all sin in the everlasting righteousness that He brought in—in the perpetual intercession that He carries on as our Representative at God's right hand—in His power to save to the uttermost the chief of sinners, His willingness to receive and pardon the vilest, His readiness to bear with the weakest—in the grace of the Holy Spirit, which He plants in the hearts of all His people, renewing, sanctifying, and causing old things to pass away and all things to become new—in all this—and oh, what a brief sketch it is!—in all this, I say, there is a full, perfect, and complete medicine for the hideous disease of sin. Awful and tremendous as the right view of sin undoubtedly is, no one need faint and despair if he will take a right view of Jesus Christ at the same time. No wonder Flavel ends many a chapter of his admirable *Fountain of Life* with the touching words, "Blessed be God for Jesus Christ."

In bringing this mighty subject to a close, I feel that I have only touched the surface of it. It is one that cannot be thoroughly handled in a chapter like this. He who would see it treated fully and exhaustively must turn to such masters of experimental theology as Owen, and Burgess, and Manton, and Charnock, and the other giants of the Puritan school. On subjects like this there are no writers to be compared to the Puritans. It only remains for me to point out some practical uses to which the whole doctrine of sin may be profitably turned in the present day.

(a) I say, then, in the first place, that a scriptural view of sin is one of the *best antidotes to that vague, dim, misty, hazy kind of theology* that is so painfully current in the present age. It is vain to shut our eyes to the fact that there is a vast quantity of so-called Christianity nowadays that you cannot declare positively unsound, but which, nevertheless, is not full measure, good weight, and sixteen ounces to the pound. It is a Christianity in which there is undeniably "something about Christ, and something about grace, and something about faith, and something about repentance, and something about holiness"; but it is not the real "thing as it is" in the Bible. Things are out of place, and out of proportion. As old Latimer would have said, it is a kind of "mingle-mangle," and does no good. It neither exercises influence on daily conduct, nor comforts in life, nor gives peace in death; and those who hold it often awake too late to find that they have got nothing solid under their feet. Now I believe the likeliest way to cure and mend this defective kind of religion is to bring forward more prominently the old scriptural truth about the sinfulness of sin. People will never set their faces decidedly toward heaven, and live like pilgrims, until they really feel that they are in danger of hell. Let us all try to revive the old teaching about sin, in nurseries, in schools, in training colleges, in universities. Let us not forget that "the law is good if we use it lawfully," and that "by the law is the knowledge of sin" (1 Tim. 1:8; Rom. 3:20; 7:7). Let us bring the law to the front and press it on men's attention. Let us expound and beat out the Ten Commandments, and show the length, and breadth, and depth, and height of their requirements. This is the way of our Lord in the Sermon on the Mount. We cannot do better than follow His plan. We may depend upon it, men will never come to Jesus, and stay with Jesus, and live for Jesus, unless they really know why they are to come, and what is their need. Those whom the Spirit draws to Jesus are those whom the Spirit has convinced of sin. Without thorough conviction of sin, men may seem to come to Jesus and follow Him for a season, but they will soon fall away and return to the world.

(b) In the next place, a scriptural view of sin is one of the *best antidotes to the extravagantly broad and liberal theology* that is so much in vogue at the present time. The tendency of modern thought is to reject dogmas, creeds, and every kind of bounds in religion. It is thought grand and wise to condemn no opinion whatsoever, and to pronounce all earnest and clever teachers to be trustworthy, however heterogeneous and mutually destructive their opinions may be. Everything forsooth is true, and nothing is false! Everybody is right, and nobody is wrong! Everybody is likely to be saved, and nobody is to be lost! The atonement and substitution of Christ, the personality of the devil, the miraculous element in Scripture, the reality and eternity of future punishment, all these mighty foundation stones are coolly tossed overboard, like lumber, in order to lighten the ship of Christianity, and enable it to keep pace with modern science.

Stand up for these great verities, and you are called narrow, illiberal, old-fashioned, and a theological fossil! Quote a text, and you are told that all truth is not confined to the pages of an ancient Jewish Book, and that free inquiry has found out many things since the Book was completed! Now, I know nothing so likely to counteract this modern plague as constant clear statements about the nature, reality, vileness, power, and guilt of sin. We must charge home into the consciences of these men of broad views, and demand a plain answer to some plain questions. We must ask them to lay their hands on their hearts, and tell us whether their favorite opinions comfort them in the day of sickness, in the hour of death, by the bedside of dying parents, by the grave of beloved wife or child. We must ask them whether a vague earnestness, without definite doctrine, gives them peace at seasons like these. We must challenge them to tell us whether they do not sometimes feel a gnawing "something" within, which all the free inquiry and philosophy and science in the world cannot satisfy. And then we must tell them that this gnawing "something" is the sense of sin, guilt, and corruption, which they are leaving out in their calculations. And, above all, we must tell them that nothing will ever make them feel rest, but submission to the old doctrines of man's ruin and Christ's redemption, and simple childlike faith in Jesus.

(c) In the next place, a right view of sin is the *best antidote to that sensuous, ceremonial, formal kind of Christianity*, which has swept over England like a flood in the last twenty-five years, and carried away so many before it. I can well believe that there is much that is attractive in this system of religion, to a certain order of minds, so long as the conscience is not fully enlightened. But when that wonderful part of our constitution called conscience is really awake and alive, I find it hard to believe that a sensuous, ceremonial Christianity will thoroughly satisfy us. A little child is easily quieted and amused with gaudy toys, and dolls, and rattles, so long as it is not hungry; but once let it feel the cravings of nature within, and we know that nothing will satisfy it but food. Just so it is with man in the matter of his soul. Music, and flowers, and candles, and incense, and banners, and processions, and beautiful vestments, and confessionals, and man-made ceremonies of a semi-Romish character, may do well enough for him under certain conditions. But once let him "awake and arise from the dead," and he will not rest content with these things. They will seem to him mere solemn triflings and a waste of time. Once let him see his sin, and he must see his Savior. He feels stricken with a deadly disease, and nothing will satisfy him but the great Physician. He hungers and thirsts, and he must have nothing less than the bread of life. I may seem bold in what I am about to say; but I fearlessly venture the assertion, that four-fifths of the semi-Romanism of the last quarter of a century would never have existed if English people had been taught more fully and clearly the nature, vileness, and sinfulness of sin.

(d) In the next place, a right view of sin is one of the *best antidotes to the overstrained theories of perfection*, of which we hear so much in these times. I shall say but little about this, and in saying it I trust I shall not give offense. If those who press on us perfection mean nothing more than an all-around consistency, and a careful attention to all the graces that make up the Christian character, reason would say that we should not only bear with them, but agree with them entirely. By all means let us aim high. But if men really mean to tell us that here in this world a believer can attain to entire freedom from sin, live for years in unbroken and uninterrupted communion with God, and feel for the months together not so much as one evil thought, I must honestly say that such an opinion appears to me very unscriptural. I go even further. I say that the opinion is very dangerous to him who holds it, and very likely to depress, discourage, and keep back inquirers after salvation. I cannot find the slightest warrant in God's Word for expecting such perfection as this while we are in the body. I believe the words of our Fifteenth Article are strictly true—that "Christ alone is without sin; and that all we, the rest, though baptized and born again in Christ, offend in many things; and if we say that we have no sin, we deceive ourselves, and the truth is not in us." To use the language of our first homily,

> There be imperfections in our best works: we do not love God so much as we are bound to do, with all our hearts, mind, and power; we do not fear God so much as we ought to do; we do not pray to God but with many and great imperfections. We give, forgive, believe, live, and hope imperfectly;

we speak, think, and do imperfectly; we fight against the devil, the world, and the flesh imperfectly. Let us, therefore, not be ashamed to confess plainly our state of imperfection.

Once more I repeat what I have said, the best preservative against this temporary delusion about perfection that clouds some minds—for such I hope I may call it—is a clear, full, distinct understanding of the nature, sinfulness, and deceitfulness of sin.

(e) In the last place, a scriptural view of sin will prove an admirable *antidote to the low views of personal holiness*, which are so painfully prevalent in these last days of the church. This is a very painful and delicate subject, I know; but I dare not turn away from it. It has long been my sorrowful conviction that the standard of daily life among professing Christians in this country has been gradually falling. I am afraid that Christlike love, kindness, good-temper, unselfishness, meekness, gentleness, good-nature, self-denial, zeal to do good, and separation from the world are far less appreciated than they ought to be, and than they used to be in the days of our fathers.

Into the causes of this state of things, I cannot pretend to enter fully, and can only suggest conjectures for consideration. It may be that a certain profession of religion has become so fashionable and comparatively easy in the present age, that the streams that were once narrow and deep have become wide and shallow, and what we have gained in outward show we have lost in quality. It may be that the vast increase of wealth in the last twenty-five years has insensibly introduced a plague of worldliness, and self-indulgence, and love of ease into social life. What were once called luxuries are now comforts and necessaries, and self-denial and "enduring hardness" are consequently little known. It may be that the enormous amount of controversy that marks this age has insensibly dried up our spiritual life. We have too often been content with zeal for orthodoxy, and have neglected the sober realities of daily practical godliness. Be the causes what they may, I must declare my own belief that the result remains. There has been of late years a lower standard of personal holiness among believers than there used to be in the days of our fathers. The whole result is that the Spirit is grieved! And the matter calls for much humiliation and searching of heart.

As to the best remedy for the state of things I have mentioned, I shall venture to give an opinion. Other schools of thought in the churches must judge for themselves. The cure for evangelical churchmen, I am convinced, is to be found in a clearer apprehension of the nature and sinfulness of sin. We need not go back to Egypt and borrow semi-Romish practices in order to revive our spiritual life. We need not restore the confessional, or return to monasticism or asceticism. Nothing of the kind! We must simply repent and do our first works. We must return to first principles. We must go back to "the old paths." We must sit down humbly in the presence of God, look the whole subject in the face, examine clearly what the Lord Jesus calls sin, and what the Lord Jesus calls "doing His will." We must then try to realize that it is terribly possible to live a careless, easy-going, half-worldly life, and yet at the same time to maintain evangelical principles and call ourselves evangelical people! Once let us see that sin is far viler, and far nearer to us, and sticks more closely to us than we supposed, and we shall be led, I trust and believe, to get nearer to Christ. Once drawn nearer to Christ, we shall drink more deeply out of His fullness, and learn more thoroughly to "live the life of faith" in Him, as St. Paul did. Once taught to live the life of faith in Jesus, and abiding in Him, we shall bear more fruit, shall find ourselves more strong for duty, more patient in trial, more watchful over our poor weak hearts, and more like our Master in all our little daily ways. Just in proportion as we realize how much Christ has done for us, shall we labor to do much for Christ. Much forgiven, we shall love much. In short, as the apostle says, "with open face beholding as in a glass the glory of the Lord, we are changed into the same image even as by the Spirit of the Lord" (2 Cor. 3:18).

Whatever some may please to think or say, there can be no doubt that an increased feeling about holiness is one of the signs of the times. Conferences for the promotion of "spiritual life" are becoming common in the present day. The subject of "spiritual life" finds a place on congress platforms almost every year. It has awakened an amount of interest and general attention throughout the land, for which we ought to be thankful. Any movement, based on sound principles, which helps to deepen our spiritual life and increase our personal holiness, will be a real blessing to the Church of England. It will do much to draw us together and heal our unhappy divisions. It may bring down some fresh out-pouring of the grace of the Spirit, and be "life from the dead" in these later times. But sure I am, as I said in the beginning of this chapter, we must begin low, if we would build high. I am convinced that the first step toward attaining a higher standard of holiness is to realize more fully the amazing sinfulness of sin.

1. Hooker's "Learned Discourse of Justification."

2

Sanctification

∾

"SANCTIFY THEM THROUGH THY TRUTH." *(John 17:17)*

"THIS IS THE WILL OF GOD, EVEN YOUR SANCTIFICATION." *(1 Thessalonians 4:3)*

THE SUBJECT OF SANCTIFICATION is one that many, I fear, dislike exceedingly. Some even turn from it with scorn and disdain. The very last thing they would like is to be a "saint," or a "sanctified" man. Yet the subject does not deserve to be treated in this way. It is not an enemy, but a friend.

It is a subject of the utmost importance to our souls. If the Bible be true, it is certain that unless we are "sanctified," we shall not be saved. There are three things that, according to the Bible, are absolutely necessary to the salvation of every man and woman in Christendom. These three are justification, regeneration, and sanctification. All three meet in every child of God: he is both born again, and justified, and sanctified. He who lacks any one of these three things is not a true Christian in the sight of

God, and, dying in that condition, will not be found in heaven and glorified in the last day.

It is a subject that is peculiarly seasonable in the present day. Strange doctrines have risen up of late upon the whole subject of sanctification. Some appear to confound it with justification. Others fritter it away to nothing, under the pretense of zeal for free grace, and practically neglect it altogether. Others are so much afraid of "works" being made a part of justification that they can hardly find any place at all for "works" in their religion. Others set up a wrong standard of sanctification before their eyes, and failing to attain it, waste their lives in repeated secessions from church to church, chapel to chapel, and sect to sect, in the vain hope that they will find what they want. In a day like this, a calm examination of the subject, as a great leading doctrine of the gospel, may be of great use to our souls.

I. Let us consider, firstly, *the true nature of sanctification.*

II. Let us consider, secondly, *the visible marks of sanctification.*

III. Let us consider, lastly, *wherein justification and sanctification agree and are like one another, and wherein they differ and are unlike.*

If, unhappily, the reader of these pages is one of those who care for nothing but this world, and make no profession of religion, I cannot expect him to take much interest in what I am writing. You will probably think it an affair of "words and names," and nice questions, about which it matters nothing what you hold and believe. But if you are a thoughtful, reasonable, sensible Christian, I venture to say that you will find it worthwhile to have some clear ideas about sanctification.

I. In the first place, we have to consider *the nature of sanctification.* What does the Bible mean when it speaks of a "sanctified" man?

Sanctification is that inward spiritual work that the Lord Jesus Christ works in a man by the Holy Ghost, when He calls him to be a true believer. He not only washes him from his sins in His own blood, but He also separates him from his natural love of sin and the world, puts a new principle in his heart, and makes him practically godly in life. The instrument by which the Spirit effects this work is generally the Word of God, though he sometimes uses afflictions and providential visitations "without the word" (1 Pet. 3:1). The subject of this work of Christ by His Spirit is called in Scripture a "sanctified" man.[1]

He who supposes that Jesus Christ only lived and died and rose again in order to provide justification and forgiveness of sins for His people, has yet much to learn. Whether he knows it or not, he is dishonoring our blessed Lord, and making Him only a half Savior. The Lord Jesus has undertaken everything that His people's souls require; not only to deliver them from the guilt of their sins by His atoning death, but from the dominion of their sins, by placing in their hearts the Holy Spirit; not only to justify them, but also to sanctify them. He is, thus, not only their "righteousness," but their "sanctification" (1 Cor. 1:30). Let us hear what the Bible says: "For their sakes I sanctify myself, that they also might be sanctified." "Christ loved the church, and gave himself for it; that he might sanctify and cleanse it." "Christ gave himself for us, that he might redeem us from all iniquity, and purify unto himself a peculiar people, zealous of good works." "Christ bore our sins in his own body on the tree, that we, being dead to sins, should live unto righteousness." "Christ hath reconciled [you] in the body of his flesh through death, to present you holy and unblameable and unreproveable in his sight" (John 17:19; Eph. 5:25–26; Titus 2:14; 1 Pet. 2:24; Col. 1:21–22). Let the meaning of these five texts be carefully considered. If words mean anything, they teach that Christ undertakes the sanctification, no less than the justification, of His believing people. Both are alike provided for in that "everlasting covenant ordered in all things and sure," of which the Mediator is Christ. In fact, Christ in one place is called "he that sanctifieth," and His people, "they who are sanctified" (Heb. 2:11).

The subject before us is of such deep and vast importance that it requires fencing, guarding, clearing up, and marking out on every side. A doctrine that is needful to salvation can never be too sharply developed, or brought too fully into light. To clear away the confusion between doctrines and doctrines, which is so unhappily common among Christians, and to map out the precise relation between truths and truths in religion, is one way to attain accuracy in our theology. I shall therefore not hesitate to lay before my readers a series of connected propositions or statements, drawn from Scripture, which I think will be found useful in defining the exact nature of sanctification.

(a) Sanctification, then, is the invariable result of that *vital union with Christ that true faith gives to a Christian.* "He that abideth in me, and I in him, the same bringeth forth much fruit" (John 15:5). The branch that bears no fruit is no living branch of the vine. The union with Christ that produces no effect on heart and life is a mere formal union, which is worthless before God. The faith that has not a sanctifying influence on the character is no better than the faith of devils. It is a "dead faith, because it is alone." It is not the gift of God. It is not the faith of God's elect. In short, where there is no sanctification of life, there is no real faith in Christ. True faith works by love. It constrains a man to live unto the Lord from a deep sense of gratitude for redemption. It makes him feel that he can never do too much for Him who died for him. Being much forgiven, he loves much. He whom the blood cleanses, walks in the light. He who has real lively hope in Christ, purifies himself even as he [Christ] is pure (James 2:17–20; Titus 1:1; Gal. 5:6; 1 John 1:7; 3:3).

(b) Sanctification, again, is *the outcome and inseparable consequence of regeneration.* He who is born again and made a new creature, receives a new nature and a new principle, and always lives a new life. A regeneration that a man can have, and yet live carelessly in sin or worldliness, is a regeneration invented by uninspired theologians, but never mentioned in Scripture. On the contrary, St. John expressly says that "he that is born of God doth not commit sin—doeth righteousness—loveth the brethren—keepeth himself—and overcometh the world" (1 John 2:29; 3:9–14; 5:4–18). In a word, where there is no sanctification there is no regeneration, and where there is no holy life there is no new birth. This is, no doubt, a hard saying to many minds; but, hard or not, it is simple Bible truth. It is written plainly, that he who is born of God is one whose "seed remaineth in him, and he cannot sin, because he is born of God" (1 John 3:9).

(c) Sanctification, again, is *the only certain evidence of that indwelling of the Holy Spirit, which is essential to salvation.* "If any man have not the Spirit of Christ, he is none of his" (Rom. 8:9). The Spirit never lies dormant and idle within the soul: He always makes His presence known by the fruit He causes to be borne in heart, character, and life. "The fruit of the Spirit," says St. Paul, "is love, joy, peace, longsuffering, gentleness, goodness, faith, meekness, temperance," and such like (Gal. 5:22–23). Where these things are to be found, there is the Spirit: where these things are wanting, men are dead before God. The Spirit is compared to the wind, and, like the wind, He cannot be seen by our bodily eyes. But just as we know there is a wind by the effect it produces on waves, and trees, and smoke, so we may know the Spirit is in a man by the effects He produces in the man's conduct. It is nonsense to suppose that we have the Spirit, if we do not also "walk in the Spirit" (Gal. 5:25). We may depend on it as a positive certainty, that where there is no holy living, there is no Holy Ghost. The seal that the Spirit stamps on Christ's people is sanctification. As many as are actually "led by the Spirit of God, they," and they only, "are the sons of God" (Rom. 8:14).

(d) Sanctification, again, is *the only sure mark of God's election.* The names and number of the elect are a secret thing, no doubt, which God has wisely kept in His own power, and not revealed to man. It is not given to us in this world to study the pages of the Book of Life, and see if our names are there. But if there is one thing clearly and plainly laid down about election, it is this—that elect men and women may be known and distinguished by holy lives. It is expressly written that they are "elect through sanctification—chosen unto salvation through sanctification—predestinated to be conformed to the image of God's Son—and chosen in Christ before the foundation of the world that they should be holy." Hence, when St. Paul saw the working "faith" and laboring "love" and patient "hope" of the Thessalonian believers, he says, "I know your election of God" (1 Pet. 1:2; 2 Thess. 2:13; Rom. 8:29; Eph. 1:4; 1 Thess. 1:3–4). He who boasts of being one of God's elect, while he is willfully and habitually living in sin, is only deceiving himself, and talking wicked blasphemy. Of course it is hard to know what people really are, and many who make a fair show outwardly in religion may turn out at last to be rotten-hearted hypocrites. But where there is not, at least, some appearance of sanctification, we may be quite certain there is no election. The Church Catechism correctly and wisely teaches that the Holy Ghost "sanctifieth all the elect people of God."

(e) Sanctification, again, *is a thing that will always be seen.* Like the great Head of the church, from whom it springs, it "cannot be hid." "Every tree is known by his own fruit" (Luke 6:44). A truly sanctified person may be so clothed with humility, that he can see in himself nothing but infirmity and defects. Like Moses, when he came down from the Mount, he may not be conscious that his face shines. Like the righteous, in the mighty parable of the sheep and the goats, he may not see that he has done anything worthy of his Master's notice and commendation: "When saw we thee an hungered, and fed thee?" (Matt. 25:37). But whether he sees it himself or not, others will always see in him a tone, and taste, and character, and habit of life unlike that of other men. The very idea of a man being "sanctified," while no holiness can be seen in his life, is flat nonsense and a misuse of words. Light may be very dim; but if there is only a spark in a dark room, it will be seen. Life may be very feeble; but if the pulse only beats a little, it will be felt. It is just the same with a sanctified man: his sanctification will be something felt and seen, though he himself may not understand it. A "saint" in whom nothing can be seen but worldliness or sin is a kind of monster not recognized in the Bible!

(f) Sanctification, again, is *a thing for which every believer is responsible.* In saying this I would not be mistaken. I hold as strongly as anyone that every man on earth is accountable to

God, and that all the lost will be speechless and without excuse at the last day. Every man has power to "lose his own soul" (Matt. 16:26). But while I hold this, I maintain that believers are eminently and peculiarly responsible, and under a special obligation to live holy lives. They are not as others, dead and blind and unrenewed: they are alive unto God, and have light and knowledge, and a new principle within them. Whose fault is it if they are not holy, but their own? On whom can they throw the blame if they are not sanctified, but themselves? God, who has given them grace and a new heart, and a new nature, has deprived them of all excuse if they do not live for His praise. This is a point that is far too much forgotten. A man who professes to be a true Christian, while he sits still, content with a very low degree of sanctification (if indeed he has any at all), and coolly tells you he "can do nothing," is a very pitiable sight and a very ignorant man. Against this delusion let us watch and be on our guard. The Word of God always addresses its precepts to believers as accountable and responsible beings. If the Savior of sinners gives us renewing grace, and calls us by His Spirit, we may be sure that He expects us to use our grace, and not to go to sleep. It is forgetfulness of this that causes many believers to "grieve the Holy Spirit," and makes them very useless and uncomfortable Christians.

(g) Sanctification, again, is *a thing which admits of growth and degrees.* A man may climb from one step to another in holiness, and be far more sanctified at one period of his life than another. More pardoned and more justified than he is when he first believes, he cannot be, though he may feel it more. More sanctified he certainly may be, because every grace in his new character may be strengthened, enlarged, and deepened. This is the evident meaning of our Lord's last prayer for His disciples, when He used the words, "Sanctify them"; and of St. Paul's prayer for the Thessalonians, "The very God of peace sanctify you" (John 17:17; 1 Thess. 5:23). In both cases the expression plainly implies the possibility of increased sanctification; while such an expression as "justify them" is never once in Scripture applied to a believer, because he cannot be more justified than he is. I can find no warrant in Scripture for the doctrine of "imputed sanctification." It is a doctrine that seems to me to confuse things that differ, and to lead to very evil consequences. Not least, it is a doctrine that is flatly contradicted by the experience of all the most eminent Christians. If there is any point on which God's holiest saints agree it is this: that they see more, and know more, and feel more, and do more, and repent more, and believe more, as they get on in spiritual life, and in proportion to the closeness of their walk with God. In short, they "grow in grace," as St. Peter exhorts believers to do; and "abound more and more," according to the words of St. Paul (2 Pet. 3:18; 1 Thess. 4:1).

(h) Sanctification, again, is *a thing that depends greatly on a diligent use of scriptural means.* When I speak of "means," I have in view Bible reading, private prayer, regular attendance on public worship, regular hearing of God's Word, and regular reception of the Lord's Supper. I lay it down as a simple matter of fact, that no one who is careless about such things must ever expect to make much progress in sanctification. I can find no record of any eminent saint who ever neglected them. They are appointed channels through which the Holy Spirit conveys fresh supplies of grace to the soul, and strengthens the work that He has begun in the inward man. Let men call this legal doctrine if they please, but I will never shrink from declaring my belief that there are no "spiritual gains without pains." I should as soon expect a farmer to prosper in business who contented himself with sowing his fields and never looking at them till harvest, as expect a believer to attain much holiness who was not diligent about his Bible reading, his prayers, and the use of his Sundays. Our God is a God who works by means, and He will never bless the soul of that man who pretends to be so high and spiritual that he can get on without them.

(i) Sanctification, again, is *a thing that does not prevent a man having a great deal of inward spiritual conflict.* By conflict I mean a struggle within the heart between the old nature and the new, the flesh and the spirit, which are to be found together in every believer (Gal. 5:17). A deep sense of that struggle, and a vast amount of mental discomfort from it, are no proof that a man is not sanctified. Nay, rather, I believe they are healthy symptoms of our condition, and prove that we are not dead, but alive. A true Christian is one who has not only peace of conscience, but war within. He may be known by his warfare as well as by his peace. In saying this, I do not forget that I am contradicting the views of some well-meaning Christians, who hold the doctrine called "sinless perfection." I cannot help that. I believe that what I say is confirmed by the language of St. Paul in the seventh chapter of Romans. That chapter I commend to the careful study of all my readers. I am quite satisfied that it does not describe the experience of an unconverted man, or of a young and unestablished Christian; but of an old, experienced saint in close communion with God. None but such a man could say, "I delight in the law of God after the inward man" (Rom. 7:22). I believe, furthermore, that what I say is proved by the experience of all the most eminent servants of Christ who have ever lived. The full proof is to be seen in their journals, their autobiographies, and their lives. Believing all this, I shall never hesitate to tell people that inward conflict is no proof that a man is not holy, and that they must not think they are not sanctified because they do not feel entirely free from inward struggle. Such freedom we shall doubtless have in heaven; but we shall never enjoy it in this world. The heart of the best Christian, even at his best, is a field occupied by two rival camps, and the "company of two armies" (Song of Sol. 6:13). Let the words of the Thirteenth and Fifteenth Articles be well considered by all churchmen: "The infection of nature doth remain in them that are regenerated." "Although baptized and born again in Christ, we offend in many things; and if we say that we have no sin, we deceive ourselves, and the truth is not in us."[2]

(j) Sanctification, again, is *a thing that cannot justify a man, and yet it pleases God.* This may seem wonderful, and yet it is true. The holiest actions of the holiest saint who ever lived are all more or less full of defects and imperfections. They are either wrong in their motive or defective in their performance, and in themselves are nothing better than "splendid sins," deserving God's wrath and condemnation. To suppose that such actions can stand the severity of God's judgment, atone for sin, and merit heaven, is simply absurd. "By the deeds of the law shall no flesh be justified." "We conclude that a man is justified by faith without the deeds of the law" (Rom. 3:20–28). The only righteousness in which we can appear before God is the righteousness of another —even the perfect righteousness of our Substitute and Representative, Jesus Christ the Lord. His work, and not our work, is our only title to heaven. This is a truth that we should be ready to die to maintain. For all this, however, the Bible distinctly teaches that the holy actions of a sanctified man, although imperfect, are pleasing in the sight of God. "With such sacrifices God is well pleased" (Heb. 13:16). "Obey your parents, for this is well pleasing to the Lord" (Col. 3:20). "We do those things that are pleasing in his sight" (1 John 3:22). Let this never be forgotten, for it is a very comfortable doctrine. Just as a parent is pleased with the efforts of his little child to please him, though it be only by picking a daisy or walking across a room, so is our Father in heaven pleased with the poor performances of His believing children. He looks at the motive, principle, and intention of their actions, and not merely at their quantity and quality. He regards them as members of His own dear Son, and for His sake, wherever there is a single eye, He is well pleased. Those churchmen who dispute this would do well to study the Twelfth Article of the Church of England.

(k) Sanctification, again, is *a thing that will be found absolutely necessary as a witness to our character in the great day of judgment.* It will be utterly useless to plead that we believed in Christ, unless our faith has had some sanctifying effect and been seen in our lives. Evidence, evidence, evidence, will be the one thing wanted when the great white throne is set, when the books are opened, when the graves give up their tenants, when the dead are arraigned before the bar of God. Without some evidence that our faith in Christ was real and genuine, we shall only rise again to be condemned. I can find no evidence that will be admitted in that day, except sanctification. The question will not be how we talked and what we professed, but how we lived and what we did. Let no man deceive himself on this point. If anything is certain about the future, it is certain that there will be a judgment; and if anything is certain about judgment, it is certain that men's "works" and "doings" will be considered and examined in it (John 5:29; 2 Cor. 5:10; Rev. 20:13). He who supposes works are of no importance, because they cannot justify us, is a very ignorant Christian. Unless he opens his eyes, he will find to his cost that if he comes to the bar of God without some evidence of grace, he had better never have been born.

(l) Sanctification, in the last place, is *absolutely necessary in order to train and prepare us for heaven.* Most men hope to go to heaven when they die; but few, it may be feared, take the trouble to consider whether they would enjoy heaven if they got there. Heaven is essentially a holy place; its inhabitants are all holy; its occupations are all holy. To be really happy in heaven, it is clear and plain that we must be somewhat trained and made ready for heaven while we are on earth. The notion of a purgatory after death, which shall turn sinners into saints, is a lying invention of man, and is nowhere taught in the Bible. We must be saints before we die, if we are to be saints afterward in glory. The favorite idea of many, that dying men need nothing except absolution and forgiveness of sins to fit them for their great change, is a profound delusion. We need the work of the Holy Spirit as well as the work of Christ; we need renewal of the heart as well as the atoning blood; we need to be sanctified as well as to be justified. It is common to hear people saying on their deathbeds, "I only want the Lord to forgive me my sins, and take me to rest." But those who say such things forget that the rest of heaven would be utterly useless if we had no heart to enjoy it! What could an unsanctified man do in heaven, if by any chance he got there? Let that question be fairly looked in the face, and fairly answered. No man can possibly be happy in a place where he is not in his element, and where all around him is not congenial to his tastes, habits, and character. When an eagle is happy in an iron cage, when a sheep is happy in the water, when an owl is happy in the blaze of noonday sun, when a fish is happy on the dry land—then, and not till then, will I admit that the unsanctified man could be happy in heaven.[3]

I lay down these twelve propositions about sanctification with a firm persuasion that they are true, and I ask all who read these pages to ponder them well. Each of them would admit of being expanded and handled more fully, and all of them deserve private thought and consideration. Some of them may be disputed and contradicted; but I doubt whether any of them can be overthrown or proved untrue. I only ask for them a fair and impartial hearing. I believe in my conscience that they are likely to assist men in attaining clear views of sanctification.

II. I now proceed to take up the second point that I proposed to consider. That point is the *visible evidence of sanctification.* In a word, what are the visible marks of a sanctified man? What may we expect to see in him?

This is a very wide and difficult department of our subject. It is wide, because it necessitates the mention of many details that cannot be handled fully in the limits of a chapter like this. It is difficult, because it cannot possibly be treated without giving offense. But at any risk, truth ought to be spoken; and there is some kind of truth that especially requires to be spoken in the present day.

(**a**) True sanctification then does not consist in *talk about religion.* This is a point that ought never to be forgotten. The vast increase of education and preaching in these latter days makes it absolutely necessary to raise a warning voice. People hear so much of gospel truth that they contract an unholy familiarity with its words and phrases, and sometimes talk so fluently about its doctrines that you might think them true Christians. In fact it is sickening and disgusting to hear the cool and flippant language that many pour out about "conversion—the Savior—the gospel—finding peace—free grace," and the like, while they are notoriously serving sin or living for the world. Can we doubt that such talk is abominable in God's sight, and is little better than cursing, swearing, and taking God's name in vain? The tongue is not the only member that Christ bids us give to His service. God does not want His people to be mere empty tubs, sounding brass, and tinkling cymbals. We must be sanctified, not only "in word and in tongue, but in deed and truth" (1 John 3:18).

(b) True sanctification does not consist in *temporary religious feelings*. This again is a point about which a warning is greatly needed. Mission services and revival meetings are attracting great attention in every part of the land, and producing a great sensation. The Church of England seems to have taken a new lease of life and exhibits a new activity; and we ought to thank God for it. But these things have their attendant dangers as well as their advantages. Wherever wheat is sown, the devil is sure to sow tares. Many, it may be feared, appear moved and touched and roused under the preaching of the gospel, while in reality their hearts are not changed at all. A kind of animal excitement from the contagion of seeing others weeping, rejoicing, or affected, is the true account of their case. Their wounds are only skin deep, and the peace they profess to feel is skin deep also. Like the stony-ground hearers, they "receive the Word with joy" (Matt.

13:20); but after a little they fall away, go back to the world, and are harder and worse than before. Like Jonah's gourd, they come up suddenly in a night and perish in a night. Let these things not be forgotten. Let us beware in this day of healing wounds slightly, and crying, Peace, peace, when there is no peace. Let us urge on everyone who exhibits new interest in religion to be content with nothing short of the deep, solid, sanctifying work of the Holy Ghost. Reaction, after false religious excitement, is a most deadly disease of soul. When the devil is only temporarily cast out of a man in the heat of a revival, and by and by returns to his house, the last state becomes worse than the first. Better a thousand times begin more slowly, and then "continue in the word" steadfastly, than begin in a hurry, without counting the cost, and by and by look back, with Lot's wife, and return to the world. I declare I know no state of soul more dangerous than to imagine we are born again and sanctified by the Holy Ghost, because we have picked up a few religious feelings.

(c) True sanctification does not consist in *outward formalism and external devoutness*. This is an enormous delusion, but unhappily a very common one. Thousands appear to imagine that true holiness is to be seen in an excessive quantity of bodily religion—in constant attendance on church services, reception of the Lord's Supper, and observance of fasts and saints' days—in multiplied bowings and turnings and gestures and postures during public worship—in self-imposed austerities and petty self-denials —in wearing peculiar dresses, and the use of pictures and crosses.

I freely admit that some people take up these things from conscientious motives, and actually believe that they help their souls. But I am afraid that in many cases this external religiousness is made a substitute for inward holiness; and I am quite certain that it falls utterly short of sanctification of heart. Above all, when I see that many followers of this outward, sensuous, and formal style of Christianity are absorbed in worldliness, and plunge headlong into its pomps and vanities, without shame, I feel that there is need of very plain speaking on the subject. There may be an immense amount of "bodily service," while there is not a jot of real sanctification.

(d) Sanctification does not consist in *retirement from our place in life, and the renunciation of our social duties.* In every age it has been a snare with many to take up this line in the pursuit of holiness. Hundreds of hermits have buried themselves in some wilderness, and thousands of men and women have shut themselves up within the walls of monasteries and convents, under the vain idea that by so doing they would escape sin and become eminently holy. They have forgotten that no bolts and bars can keep out the devil, and that, wherever we go, we carry that root of all evil, our own hearts. To become a monk, or a nun, or to join a House of Mercy, is not the high road to sanctification. True holiness does not make a Christian evade difficulties, but face and overcome them. Christ would have His people show that His grace is not a mere hothouse plant, which can only thrive under shelter, but a strong, hardy thing, which can flourish in every relation of life. It is doing our duty in that state to which God has called us—like salt in the midst of corruption, and light in the midst of darkness—which is a primary element in sanctification. It is not the man who hides himself in a cave, but the man who glorifies God as master or servant, parent or child, in the family and in the street, in business and in trade, who is the scriptural type of a sanctified man. Our Master Himself said in His last prayer, "I pray not that thou shouldest take them out of the world, but that thou shouldest keep them from the evil" (John 17:15).

(e) Sanctification does not consist in *the occasional performance of right actions.* It is the habitual working of a new heavenly principle within, which runs through all a man's daily conduct, both in great things and in small. Its seat is in the heart, and like the heart in the body, it has a regular influence on every part of the character. It is not like a pump, which only sends forth water when worked upon from without, but like a perpetual fountain, from which a stream is ever flowing spontaneously and naturally. Even Herod, when he heard John the Baptist, "did many things," while his heart was utterly wrong in the sight of God (Mark 6:20). Just so there are scores of people in the present day who seem to have spasmodical fits of "goodness," as it is called, and do many right things under the influence of sickness, affliction, death in the family, public calamities, or a sudden qualm of conscience. Yet all the time any intelligent observer can see plainly that they are not converted, and that they know nothing of "sanctification." A true saint, like Hezekiah, will be wholehearted. He will "count God's commandments concerning all things to be right, and hate every false way" (2 Chron. 31:21; Ps. 119:104).

(f) Genuine sanctification will show itself in *habitual respect to God's law, and habitual effort to live in obedience to it as the rule of life.* There is no greater mistake than to suppose that a Christian has nothing to do with the law and the Ten Commandments, because he cannot be justified by keeping them. The same Holy Ghost who convinces the believer of sin by the law, and leads him to Christ for justification, will always lead him to a spiritual use of the law, as a friendly guide, in the pursuit of sanctification. Our Lord Jesus Christ never made light of the Ten Commandments; on the contrary, in His first public discourse, the Sermon on the Mount, He expounded them, and showed the searching nature of their requirements. St. Paul never made light of the law: on the contrary, he says, "The law is good, if a man use it lawfully." "I delight in the law of God after the inward man" (1 Tim. 1:8; Rom. 7:22). He who pretends to be a saint, while he sneers at the Ten Commandments, and thinks nothing of lying, hypocrisy, swindling, ill-temper, slander, drunkenness, and breach of the Seventh Commandment, is under a fearful delusion. He will find it hard to prove that he is a "saint" in the last day!

(g) Genuine sanctification will show itself in a *habitual endeavor to do Christ's will, and to live by His practical precepts.*

These precepts are to be found scattered everywhere throughout the four Gospels, and especially in the Sermon on the Mount. He who supposes they were spoken without the intention of promoting holiness, and that a Christian need not attend to them in his daily life, is really little better than a lunatic, and at any rate is a grossly ignorant person. To hear some men talk, and read some men's writings, one might imagine that our blessed Lord, when He was on earth, never taught anything but doctrine, and left practical duties to be taught by others! The slightest knowledge of the four Gospels ought to tell us that this is a complete mistake. What His disciples ought to be and to do is continually brought forward in our Lord's teaching. A truly sanctified man will never forget this. He serves a Master who said, "Ye are my friends if ye do whatsoever I command you" (John 15:14).

(h) Genuine sanctification will show itself in a *habitual desire to live up to the standard that St. Paul sets before the churches in his writings.* That standard is to be found in the closing chapters of nearly all his Epistles. The common idea of many persons that St. Paul's writings are full of nothing but doctrinal statements and controversial subjects—justification, election, predestination, prophecy, and the like —is an entire delusion, and a melancholy proof of the ignorance of Scripture that prevails in these latter days. I defy anyone to read St. Paul's writings carefully without finding in them a large quantity of plain, practical directions about the Christian's duty in every relation of life, and about our daily habits, temper, and behavior to one another.

These directions were written down by inspiration of God for the perpetual guidance of professing Christians. He who does not attend to them may possibly pass muster as a member of a church or a chapel, but he certainly is not what the Bible calls a "sanctified" man.

(i) Genuine sanctification will show itself in *habitual attention to the active graces, which our Lord so beautifully exemplified, and especially to the grace of charity.* "A new commandment I give unto you, that ye love one another; as I have loved you, that ye also love one another. By this shall all men know that ye are my disciples, if ye have love one to another" (John 13:34–35). A sanctified man will try to do good in the world, and to lessen the sorrow and increase the happiness of all around him. He will aim to be like his Master, full of kindness and love to everyone; and this not in word only, by calling people "dear," but by deeds and actions and self-denying work, according as he has opportunity. The selfish Christian professor, who wraps himself up in his own conceit of superior knowledge, and seems to care nothing whether others sink or swim, go to heaven or hell, so long as he walks to church or chapel in his Sunday best, and is called a "sound member"—such a man knows nothing of sanctification. He may think himself a saint on earth, but he will not be a saint in heaven. Christ will never be found the Savior of those who know nothing of following His example. Saving faith and real converting grace will always produce some conformity to the image of Jesus (Col. 3:10).[4]

(j) Genuine sanctification, in the last place, will show itself in *habitual attention to the passive graces of Christianity.* When I speak of passive graces, I mean those graces that are especially shown in submission to the will of God, and in bearing and for-bearing toward one another. Few people, perhaps, unless they have examined the point, have an idea how much is said about these graces in the New Testament, and how important a place they seem to fill. This is the special point that St. Peter dwells upon in commending our Lord Jesus Christ's example to our notice: "Christ also suffered for us, leaving us an example, that we should follow his steps: who did no sin, neither was guile found in his mouth: who, when he was reviled, reviled not again; when he suffered, he threatened not; but committed himself to him that judgeth righteously" (1 Pet. 2:21–23). This is the one piece of profession that the Lord's Prayer requires us to make: "Forgive us our trespasses, as we forgive them that trespass against us"; and the one point that is commented upon at the end of the prayer. This is the point that occupies one-third of the list of the fruits of the Spirit, supplied by St. Paul. Nine are named, and three of these, "longsuffering, gentleness, and meekness," are unquestionably passive graces (Gal. 5:22–23). I must plainly say that I do not think this subject is sufficiently considered by Christians. The passive graces are no doubt harder to attain than the active ones, but they are precisely the graces that have the greatest influence on the world. Of one thing I feel very sure—it is nonsense to pretend to sanctification unless we follow after the meekness, gentleness, longsuffering, and forgiveness of which the Bible makes so much. People who are habitually giving way to peevish and cross tempers in daily life, and are constantly sharp with their tongues, and disagreeable to all around them— spiteful people, vindictive people, revengeful people, malicious people—of whom, alas, the world is only too full! —all such know little, as they should know, about sanctification.

Such are the visible marks of a sanctified man. I do not say that they are all to be seen equally in all God's people. I freely admit that in the best they are not fully and perfectly exhibited. But I do say confidently, that the things of which I have been speaking are the scriptural marks of sanctification, and that they who know nothing of them may well doubt whether they have any grace at all. Whatever others may please to say, I will never shrink from saying that genuine sanctification is a thing that can be seen, and that the marks I have endeavored to sketch out are more or less the marks of a sanctified man.

III. I now propose to consider, in the last place, *the distinction between justification and sanctification.* Wherein do they agree, and wherein do they differ? This branch of our subject is one of great importance, though I fear it will not seem so to all my readers. I shall handle it briefly, but I dare not pass it over altogether. Too many are apt to look at nothing but the surface of things in religion, and regard nice distinctions in theology as questions of "words and names," which are of little real value. But I warn all who are in earnest about their souls, that the discomfort that arises from not "distinguishing things that differ" in Christian doctrine is very great indeed; and I especially advise them, if they love peace, to seek clear views about the matter before us. Justification and sanctification are two distinct things we must always remember. Yet there are points in which they agree and points in which they differ. Let us try to find out what they are.

In what, then, are justification and sanctification alike?

(a) Both proceed originally from the free grace of God. It is of His gift alone that believers are justified or sanctified at all.

(b) Both are part of that great work of salvation that Christ, in the eternal covenant, has undertaken on behalf of His people. Christ is the fountain of life, from which pardon and holiness both flow. The root of each is Christ.

(c) Both are to be found in the same persons. Those who are justified are always sanctified, and those who are sanctified are always justified. God has joined them together, and they cannot be put asunder.

(d) Both begin at the same time. The moment a person begins to be a justified person, he also begins to be a sanctified person. He may not feel it, but it is a fact.

(e) Both are alike necessary to salvation. No one ever reached heaven without a renewed heart as well as forgiveness, without the Spirit's grace as well as the blood of Christ, without a meetness for eternal glory as well as a title. The one is just as necessary as the other.

Such are the points on which justification and sanctification agree. Let us now reverse the picture, and see wherein they differ.

(a) Justification is the reckoning and counting a man to be righteous for the sake of another, even Jesus Christ the Lord. Sanctification is the actual making a man inwardly righteous, though it may be in a very feeble degree.

(b) The righteousness we have by our justification is not our own, but the everlasting perfect righteousness of our great Mediator Christ, imputed to us, and made our own by faith. The righteousness we have by sanctification is our own righteousness, imparted, inherent, and wrought in us by the Holy Spirit, but mingled with much infirmity and imperfection.

(c) In justification our own works have no place at all, and simple faith in Christ is the one thing needful. In sanctification our own works are of vast importance and God bids us fight, and watch, and pray, and strive, and take pains, and labor.

(d) Justification is a finished and complete work, and a man is perfectly justified the moment he believes. Sanctification is an imperfect work, comparatively, and will never be perfected until we reach heaven.

(e) Justification admits of no growth or increase: a man is as much justified the hour he first comes to Christ by faith as he will be to all eternity. Sanctification is eminently a progressive work, and admits of continual growth and enlargement so long as a man lives.

(f) Justification has special reference to our persons, our

standing in God's sight, and our deliverance from guilt. Sanctification has special reference to our natures, and the moral renewal of our hearts.

(g) Justification gives us our title to heaven, and boldness to enter in. Sanctification gives us our meetness for heaven, and prepares us to enjoy it when we dwell there.

(h) Justification is the act of God about us, and is not easily discerned by others. Sanctification is the work of God within us, and cannot be hid in its outward manifestation from the eyes of men.

I commend these distinctions to the attention of all my readers, and I ask them to ponder them well. I am persuaded that one great cause of the darkness and uncomfortable feelings of many well-meaning people in the matter of religion is their habit of confounding, and not distinguishing, justification and sanctification. It can never be too strongly impressed on our minds that they are two separate things. No doubt they cannot be divided, and everyone who is a partaker of either is a partaker of both. But never, never ought they to be confounded, and never ought the distinction between them to be forgotten.

It only remains for me now to bring this subject to a conclusion by a few plain words of application. The nature and visible marks of sanctification have been brought before us. What practical reflections ought the whole matter to raise in our minds?

(1) For one thing, *let us all awake to a sense of the perilous state of many professing Christians.* "Without holiness no man

shall see the Lord"; without sanctification there is no salvation (Heb. 12:14). Then what an enormous amount of so-called religion there is which is perfectly useless! What an immense proportion of churchgoers and chapel-goers are in the broad road that leads to destruction! The thought is awful, crushing, and overwhelming. Oh, that preachers and teachers would open their eyes and realize the condition of souls around them! Oh, that men could be persuaded to "flee from the wrath to come"! If unsanctified souls can be saved and go to heaven, the Bible is not true. Yet the Bible is true and cannot lie! What must the end be!

(2) For another thing, *let us make sure work of our own condition, and never rest till we feel and know that we are "sanctified" ourselves.* What are our tastes, and choices, and likings, and inclinations? This is the great testing question. It matters little what we wish, and what we hope, and what we desire to be before we die. Where are we now? What are we doing? Are we sanctified or not? If not, the fault is all our own.

(3) For another thing, *if we would be sanctified, our course is clear and plain—we must begin with Christ.* We must go to Him as sinners, with no plea but that of utter need, and cast our souls on Him by faith, for peace and reconciliation with God. We must place ourselves in His hands, as in the hands of a good physician, and cry to Him for mercy and grace. We must wait for nothing to bring with us as a recommendation. The very first step toward sanctification, no less than justification, is to come with faith to Christ. We must first live and then work.

(4) For another thing, *if we would grow in holiness and become more sanctified, we must continually go on as we began, and be ever making fresh applications to Christ.* He is the Head from which every member must be supplied (Eph. 4:16). To live the life of daily faith in the Son of God, and to be daily drawing out of His fullness the promised grace and strength that He has laid up for His people—this is the grand secret of progressive sanctification. Believers who seem at a standstill are generally neglecting close communion with Jesus, and so grieving the Spirit. He who prayed, "Sanctify them," the last night before His crucifixion, is infinitely willing to help everyone who by faith applies to Him for help, and desires to be made more holy.

(5) For another thing, *let us not expect too much from our own hearts here below.* At our best we shall find in ourselves daily cause for humiliation, and discover that we are needy debtors to mercy and grace every hour. The more light we have, the more we shall see our own imperfection. Sinners we were when we began, sinners we shall find ourselves as we go on; renewed, pardoned, justified—yet sinners to the very last. Our absolute perfection is yet to come, and the expectation of it is one reason why we should long for heaven.

(6) Finally, *let us never be ashamed of making much of sanctification, and contending for a high standard of holiness.* While some are satisfied with a miserably low degree of attainment, and others are not ashamed to live on without any holiness at all—content with a mere round of churchgoing and chapel-going, but

never getting on, like a horse in a mill—let us stand fast in the old paths, follow after eminent holiness ourselves, and recommend it boldly to others. This is the only way to be really happy.

Let us feel convinced, whatever others may say, that holiness is happiness, and that the man who gets through life most comfortably is the sanctified man. No doubt there are some true Christians who from ill-health, or family trials, or other secret causes, enjoy little sensible comfort, and go mourning all their days on the way to heaven. But these are exceptional cases. As a general rule, in the long run of life, it will be found true that "sanctified" people are the happiest people on earth. They have solid comforts that the world can neither give nor take away. "The ways of wisdom are ways of pleasantness." "Great peace have they that love thy law." It was said by One who cannot lie, "My yoke is easy, and my burden is light." But it is also written, "There is no peace unto the wicked" (Prov 3:17; Ps. 119:165; Matt. 11:30; Isa. 48:22).

P. S.

The subject of sanctification is of such deep importance, and the mistakes made about it so many and great, that I make no apology for strongly recommending Owen, on "The Holy Spirit," to all who want to study more thoroughly the whole doctrine of sanctification. No single chapter like this can embrace it all.

I am quite aware that Owen's writings are not fashionable in the present day, and that many think fit to neglect and sneer at him as a Puritan! Yet the great divine who in Commonwealth times was dean of Christ Church, Oxford, does not deserve to be treated in this way. He had more learning and sound knowledge of Scripture in his little finger than many who depreciate him have in their whole bodies. I assert unhesitatingly that the man who wants to study experimental theology will find no books equal to those of Owen and some of his contemporaries, for complete, scriptural, and exhaustive treatment of the subjects they handle.

1. "There is mention in the Scripture of a twofold sanctification, and consequently of a twofold holiness. The first is common unto persons and things, consisting in the peculiar dedication, consecration, or separation of them unto the service of God, by his own appointment, whereby they become holy. Thus the priests and Levites of old, the ark, the altar, the tabernacle, and the temple, were sanctified and made holy; and, indeed, in all holiness whatever, there is a peculiar dedication and separation unto God. But in the sense mentioned, this was solitary and alone. No more belonged unto it but this sacred separation, nor was there any other effect of this sanctification. But, secondly, there is another kind of sanctification and holiness, wherein this separation to God is not the first thing done or intended, but a consequent and effect thereof. This is real and internal, by the communicating of a principle of holiness unto our natures, attended with its exercise in acts and duties of holy obedience unto God. This is that which we inquire after." (Owen, on "The Holy Spirit," *Works*, vol. 3, p. 370, Goold's edition.)

2. "The devil's war is better than the devil's peace. Suspect dumb holiness. When the dog is kept out of doors he howls to be let in again." "Contraries meeting, such as fire and water, conflict one with another. When Satan findeth a sanctified heart, he tempteth with much importunity. Where there is much of God and of Christ, there are strong injections and firebrands cast in at the windows, so that some of much faith have been tempted to doubt." (Rutherford's *Trial of Faith*, p. 403.)

3. "There is no imagination wherewith man is besotted, more foolish, none so pernicious, as this that persons not purified, not sanctified, not made holy in their life, should afterwards be taken into that state of blessedness which consists in

the enjoyment of God. Neither can such persons enjoy God, nor would God be a reward to them.— Holiness indeed is perfected in heaven: but the beginning of it is invariably confined to this world." (Owen, on "The Holy Spirit," p. 575, Goold's edition.)

4. "Christ in the gospel is proposed to us as our pattern and example of holiness; and as it is a cursed imagination that this was the whole end of his life and death: namely, to exemplify and confirm the doctrine of holiness which he taught—so to neglect his being our example, in considering him by faith to that end, and laboring after conformity to him, is evil and pernicious. Wherefore let us be much in the contemplation of what he was, and what he did, and how in all duties and trials he carried himself, until an image or idea of his perfect holiness is implanted in our minds, and we are made like unto him thereby." (Owen, on "The Holy Ghost," p. 513, Goold's edition.)

3

Holiness

∾

"HOLINESS, WITHOUT WHICH NO MAN SHALL SEE THE LORD."
(Hebrews 12:14)

THE TEXT that heads this page opens up a subject of deep importance. That subject is practical holiness. It suggests a question that demands the attention of all professing Christians: Are we holy? Shall we see the Lord?

That question can never be out of season. The wise man tells us, "There is a time to weep, and a time to laugh . . . a time to keep silence, and a time to speak" (Eccl. 3:4, 7); but there is no time, no, not a day, in which a man ought not to be holy. Are we?

That question concerns all ranks and conditions of men. Some are rich and some are poor—some learned and some unlearned—some masters, and some servants; but there is no rank or condition in life in which a man ought not to be holy. Are we?

I ask to be heard today about this question. How stands the account between our souls and God? In this hurrying, bustling world, let us stand still for a few minutes and consider the matter of holiness. I believe I might have chosen a subject more popular and pleasant. I am sure I might have found one more easy to handle. But I feel deeply I could not have chosen one more seasonable and more profitable to our souls. It is a solemn thing to hear the Word of God saying, "Without holiness no man shall see the Lord" (Heb. 12:14).

I shall endeavor, by God's help, to examine what true holiness is, and the reason why it is so needful. In conclusion, I shall try to point out the only way in which holiness can be attained. I have already, in the second chapter in this volume, approached this subject from a doctrinal side. Let me now try to present it to my readers in a more plain and practical point of view.

I. First, then, let me try to show *what true practical holiness is—what sort of persons are those whom God calls holy.*

A man may go great lengths, and yet never reach true holiness. It is not knowledge—Balaam had that; nor great profession—Judas Iscariot had that; nor doing many things—Herod had that; nor zeal for certain matters in religion—Jehu had that; nor morality and outward respectability of conduct—the young ruler had that; nor taking pleasure in hearing preachers—the Jews in Ezekiel's time had that; nor keeping company with godly people —Joab and Gehazi and Demas had that. Yet none of these was holy! These things alone are not holiness. A man may have any one of them, and yet never see the Lord.

What then is true practical holiness? It is a hard question to answer. I do not mean that there is any want of scriptural matter on the subject. But I fear lest I should give a defective view of holiness, and not say all that ought to be said; or lest I should say things about it that ought not to be said, and so do harm. Let me, however, try to draw a picture of holiness, that we may see it clearly before the eyes of our minds. Only let it never be forgotten, when I have said all, that my account is but a poor imperfect outline at the best.

(a) *Holiness is the habit of being of one mind with God*, according as we find His mind described in Scripture. It is the habit of agreeing in God's judgment—hating what He hates—loving what He loves—and measuring everything in this world by the standard of His Word. He who most entirely agrees with God, he is the most holy man.

(b) A holy man will *endeavor to shun every known sin, and to keep every known commandment.* He will have a decided bent of mind toward God, a hearty desire to do His will—a greater fear of displeasing Him than of displeasing the world, and a love to all His ways. He will feel what Paul felt when he said, "I delight in the law of God after the inward man" (Rom. 7:22), and what David felt when he said, "I esteem all thy precepts concerning all things to be right, and I hate every false way" (Ps. 119:128).

(c) A holy man will *strive to be like our Lord Jesus Christ.* He will not only live the life of faith in Him, and draw from Him all his daily peace and strength, but he will also labor to have the mind that was in Him, and to be "conformed to his image" (Rom.

8:29). It will be his aim to bear with and forgive others, even as Christ forgave us—to be unselfish, even as Christ pleased not Himself—to walk in love, even as Christ loved us—to be lowly minded and humble, even as Christ made Himself of no reputation and humbled Himself. He will remember that Christ was a faithful witness for the truth—that He came not to do His own will—that it was His meat and drink to do His Father's will—that He would continually deny Himself in order to minister to others —that He was meek and patient under undeserved insults—that He thought more of godly poor men than of kings—that He was full of love and compassion to sinners—that He was bold and uncompromising in denouncing sin—that He sought not the praise of men, when He might have had it—that He went about doing good—that He was separate from worldly people—that He continued instant in prayer—that He would not let even His nearest relations stand in His way when God's work was to be done. These things a holy man will try to remember. By them he will endeavor to shape his course in life. He will lay to heart the saying of John, "He that saith he abideth in Christ ought himself also so to walk, even as he walked" (1 John 2:6); and the saying of Peter, that "Christ suffered for us, leaving us an example that ye should follow his steps" (1 Pet. 2:21). Happy is he who has learned to make Christ his "all," both for salvation and example! Much time would be saved, and much sin prevented, if men would oftener ask themselves the question, "What would Christ have said and done, if He were in my place?"

(d) A holy man will *follow after meekness, longsuffering, gentleness, patience, kind tempers, government of his tongue.* He will bear much, forbear much, overlook much, and be slow to talk of standing on his rights. We see a bright example of this in the behavior of David when Shimei cursed him—and of Moses when Aaron and Miriam spoke against him (2 Sam. 16:10; Num. 12:3).

(e) A holy man will *follow after temperance and self-denial.* He will labor to mortify the desires of his body—to crucify his flesh with its affections and lusts—to curb his passions—to restrain his carnal inclinations, lest at any time they break loose. Oh, what a word is that of the Lord Jesus to the apostles, "Take heed to yourselves, lest at any time your hearts be overcharged with surfeiting and drunkenness, and cares of this life" (Luke 21:34); and that of the Apostle Paul, "I keep under my body, and bring it into subjection, lest that by any means when I have preached to others, I myself should be a castaway" (1 Cor. 9:27).

(f) A holy man will *follow after charity and brotherly kindness.* He will endeavor to observe the golden rule of doing as he would have men do to him, and speaking as he would have men speak to him. He will be full of affection toward his brethren—toward their bodies, their property, their characters, their feelings, their souls. "He that loveth another," says Paul, "hath fulfilled the law" (Rom. 13:8). He will abhor all lying, slandering, backbiting, cheating, dishonesty, and unfair dealing, even in the least things. The shekel and cubit of the sanctuary were larger than those in common use. He will strive to adorn his religion by all his outward demeanor, and to make it lovely and beautiful in the eyes of all around him. Alas, what condemning words are the thirteenth chapter of 1 Corinthians, and the Sermon on the Mount, when laid alongside the conduct of many professing Christians!

(g) A holy man will *follow after a spirit of mercy and benevolence toward others.* He will not stand all the day idle. He will not be content with doing no harm—he will try to do good. He will strive to be useful in his day and generation, and to lessen the spiritual wants and misery around him, as far as he can. Such was Dorcas, "full of good works and almsdeeds, which she did"—not merely purposed and talked about, but did. Such a one was Paul: "I will very gladly spend and be spent for you," he says, "though the more abundantly I love you the less I be loved" (Acts 9:36; 2 Cor. 12:15).

(h) A holy man will *follow after purity of heart.* He will dread all filthiness and uncleanness of spirit, and seek to avoid all things that might draw him into it. He knows his own heart is like tinder, and will diligently keep clear of the sparks of temptation. Who shall dare to talk of strength when David can fall? There is many a hint to be gleaned from the ceremonial law. Under it the man who only touched a bone, or a dead body, or a grave, or a diseased person, became at once unclean in the sight of God. And these things were emblems and figures. Few Christians are ever too watchful and too particular about this point.

(i) A holy man will *follow after the fear of God*. I do not mean the fear of a slave, who only works because he is afraid of punishment, and would be idle if he did not dread discovery. I mean rather the fear of a child, who wishes to live and move as if he was always before his father's face, because he loves him. What a noble example Nehemiah gives us of this! When he became governor at Jerusalem, he might have been chargeable to the Jews and required of them money for his support. The former governors had done so. There was none to blame him if he did. But he says, "So did not I, because of the fear of God" (Neh. 5:15).

(j) A holy man will *follow after humility*. He will desire, in lowliness of mind, to esteem all others better than himself. He will see more evil in his own heart than in any other in the world. He will understand something of Abraham's feeling, when he says, "I am dust and ashes"; and Jacob's, when he says, "I am less than the least of all thy mercies"; and Job's, when he says, "I am vile"; and Paul's, when he says, "I am chief of sinners." Holy Bradford, that faithful martyr of Christ, would sometimes finish his letters with these words, "A most miserable sinner, John Bradford." Good old Mr. Grimshaw's last words, when he lay on his deathbed, were these, "Here goes an unprofitable servant."

(k) A holy man will *follow after faithfulness in all the duties and relations in life*. He will try, not merely to fill his place as well as others who take no thought for their souls, but even better, because he has higher motives, and more help than they. Those words of Paul should never be forgotten, "Whatever ye do, do it heartily, as unto the Lord." "Not slothful in business, fervent in spirit, serving the Lord" (Col. 3:23; Rom. 12:11). Holy persons should aim at doing everything well, and should be ashamed of allowing themselves to do anything ill if they can help it. Like Daniel, they should seek to give no "occasion" against themselves, except "concerning the law of their God" (Dan. 6:5). They should strive to be good husbands and good wives, good parents and good children, good masters and good servants, good neighbors, good friends, good subjects, good in private and good in public, good in the place of business and good by their firesides. Holiness is worth little indeed, if it does not bear this kind of fruit. The Lord Jesus puts a searching question to His people, when He says, "What do ye more than others?" (Matt. 5:47).

(l) Last, but not least, a holy man will *follow after spiritual mindedness.* He will endeavor to set his affections entirely on things above, and to hold things on earth with a very loose hand. He will not neglect the business of the life that now is; but the first place in his mind and thoughts will be given to the life to come. He will aim to live like one whose treasure is in heaven, and to pass through this world like a stranger and pilgrim traveling to his home. To commune with God in prayer, in the Bible, and in the assembly of His people, these things will be the holy man's chiefest enjoyments. He will value every thing and place and company, just in proportion as it draws him nearer to God. He will enter into something of David's feeling, when he says, "My soul followeth hard after thee." "Thou art my portion" (Ps. 63:8; 119:57).

Such is the outline of holiness that I venture to sketch out. Such is the character that those who are called "holy" follow after. Such are the main features of a holy man.

But here let me say, I trust no man will misunderstand me. I am not without fear that my meaning will be mistaken, and the description I have given of holiness will discourage some tender conscience. I would not willingly make one righteous heart sad, or throw a stumbling block in any believer's way.

I do not say for a moment that holiness shuts out the presence of indwelling sin. No: far from it. It is the greatest misery of a holy man that he carries about with him a "body of death"; that often when he would do good, "evil is present with him"; that the old man is clogging all his movements, and, as it were, trying to draw him back at every step he takes (Rom. 7:21). But it is the excellence of a holy man that he is not at peace with indwelling sin, as others are. He hates it, mourns over it, and longs to be free from its company. The work of sanctification within him is like the wall of Jerusalem—the building goes forward "even in troublous times" (Dan. 9:25).

Neither do I say that holiness comes to ripeness and perfection all at once, or that these graces I have touched on must be found in full bloom and vigor before you can call a man holy. No: far from it. Sanctification is always a *progressive* work. Some men's graces are in the blade, some in the ear, and some are like full corn in the ear. All must have a beginning. We must never despise "the day of small things." And sanctification in the very best is an *imperfect* work. The history of the brightest saints who ever lived will contain many a "but," and "howbeit," and "not-withstanding," before you reach the end. The gold will never be without some dross—the light will never shine without some clouds, until we reach the heavenly Jerusalem. The sun himself has spots upon his face. The holiest men have many a blemish and defect when weighed in the balance of the sanctuary. Their life is a continual warfare with sin, the world, and the devil; and sometimes you will see them not overcoming, but overcome. The flesh is ever lusting against the spirit, and the spirit against the flesh, and "in many things they offend all" (Gal. 5:17; James 3:2).

But still, for all this, I am sure that to have such a character as I have faintly drawn, is the heart's desire and prayer of all true Christians. They press toward it, if they do not reach it. They may not attain to it, but they always aim at it. It is what they strive and labor to be, if it is not what they are.

And this I do boldly and confidently say, that true holiness is a great reality. It is something in a man that can be seen, and known, and marked, and felt by all around him. It is light: if it exists, it will show itself. It is salt: if it exists, its savor will be perceived. It is a precious ointment: if it exists, its presence cannot be hid.

I am sure we should all be ready to make allowance for much backsliding, for much occasional deadness in professing Christians. I know a road may lead from one point to another, and yet have many a winding and turn; and a man may be truly holy, and yet be drawn aside by many an infirmity. Gold is not the less gold because mingled with alloy, nor light the less light because faint and dim, nor grace the less grace because young and weak. But after every allowance, I cannot see how any man deserves to be called "holy," who willfully allows himself in sins, and is not humbled and ashamed because of them. I dare not call anyone "holy" who makes a habit of willfully neglecting known duties, and willfully doing what he knows God has commanded him not to do. Well says Owen, "I do not understand how a man can be a true believer unto whom sin is not the greatest burden, sorrow, and trouble."

Such are the leading characteristics of practical holiness. Let us examine ourselves and see whether we are acquainted with it. Let us prove our own selves.

II. Let me try, in the next place, to *show some reasons why practical holiness is so important.*

Can holiness save us? Can holiness put away sin—cover iniquities—make satisfaction for transgressions—pay our debt to God? No: not a whit. God forbid that I should ever say so. Holiness can do none of these things. The brightest saints are all "unprofitable servants." Our purest works are no better than filthy rags, when tried by the light of God's holy law. The white robe that Jesus offers, and faith puts on, must be our only righteousness—the name of Christ our only confidence—the Lamb's Book of Life our only title to heaven. With all our holiness we are no better than sinners. Our best things are stained and tainted with imperfection. They are all more or less incomplete, wrong in the motive or defective in the performance. By the deeds of the law shall no child of Adam ever be justified. "By grace are ye saved through faith, and that not of yourselves, it is the gift of God: not of works, lest any man should boast" (Eph. 2:8–9).

Why then is holiness so important? Why does the apostle say, "Without it no man shall see the Lord"? Let me set out in order a few reasons.

(a) For one thing, we must be holy, because *the voice of God in Scripture plainly commands it.* The Lord Jesus says to His people, "Except your righteousness shall exceed the righteousness of the scribes and Pharisees, ye shall in no case enter into the kingdom of heaven" (Matt. 5:20). "Be ye perfect, even as your Father which is in heaven is perfect" (Matt. 5:48). Paul tells the Thessalonians, "This is the will of God, even your sanctification" (1 Thess. 4:3). And Peter says, "As he which hath called you is holy, so be ye holy in all manner of conversation; because it is written, 'Be ye holy, for I am holy'" (1 Pet. 1:15–16). "In this," says Leighton, "law and gospel agree."

(b) We must be holy, because *this is one grand end and purpose for which Christ came into the world.* Paul writes to the Corinthians, "He died for all, that they which live should not henceforth live unto themselves, but unto him which died for them and rose again" (2 Cor. 5:15). And to the Ephesians, "Christ loved the church, and gave himself for it, that he might sanctify and cleanse it" (Eph. 5:25–26). And to Titus, "He gave himself for us, that he might redeem us from all iniquity, and purify unto himself a peculiar people, zealous of good works" (Titus 2:14). In short, to talk of men being saved from the guilt of sin, without being at the same time saved from its dominion in their hearts, is to contradict the witness of all Scripture. Are believers said to be elect?—it is "through sanctification of the Spirit." Are they predestinated?—it is "to be conformed to the image of God's Son." Are they chosen?—it is "that they may be holy." Are they called?—it is "with a holy calling." Are they afflicted?—it is that they may be "partakers of holiness." Jesus is a complete Savior. He does not merely take away the guilt of a believer's sin, He does more—He breaks its power (1 Pet. 1:2; Rom. 8:29; Eph. 1:4; 2 Tim. 1:9; Heb. 12:10).

(c) We must be holy, because *this is the only sound evidence that we have a saving faith in our Lord Jesus Christ.* The Twelfth Article of our church says truly, that "Although good works cannot put away our sins, and endure the severity of God's judgment, yet are they pleasing and acceptable to God in Christ, and do spring out necessarily of a true and lively faith, insomuch that by them a lively faith may be as evidently known as a tree discerned by its fruits." James warns us there is such a thing as a dead faith—a faith that goes no further than the profession of the lips, and has no influence on a man's character (James 2:17). True saving faith is a very different kind of thing. True faith will always show itself by its fruits—it will sanctify, it will work by love, it will overcome the world, it will purify the heart. I know that people are fond of talking about deathbed evidences. They will rest on words spoken in the hours of fear, and pain, and weakness, as if they might take comfort in them about the friends they lose. But I am afraid in ninety-nine cases out of a hundred, such evidences are not to be depended on. I suspect that, with rare exceptions, men die just as they have lived. The only safe evidence that we are one with Christ, and Christ in us, is holy life. They who live unto the Lord are generally the only people who die in the Lord. If we would die the death of the righteous, let us not rest in slothful desires only; let us seek to live His life. It is a true saying of Traill's: "That man's state is naught, and his faith unsound, that finds not his hopes of glory purifying to his heart and life."

(d) We must be holy, because *this is the only proof that we love the Lord Jesus Christ in sincerity.* This is a point on which He has spoken most plainly, in the fourteenth and fifteenth chapters of John. "If ye love me, keep my commandments." "He that hath my commandments and keepeth them, he it is that loveth me." "If a man love me, he will keep my words." "Ye are my friends if ye do whatsoever I command you" (John 14:15, 21, 23; 15:14). Plainer words than these it would be difficult to find, and woe to those who neglect them! Surely that man must be in an unhealthy state of soul who can think of all that Jesus suffered, and yet cling to those sins for which that suffering was undergone. It was sin that wove the crown of thorns—it was sin that pierced our Lord's hands, and feet, and side—it was sin that brought Him to Gethsemane and Calvary, to the cross and to the grave. Cold must our hearts be if we do not hate sin and labor to get rid of it, though we may have to cut off the right hand and pluck out the right eye in doing it.

(e) We must be holy, because *this is the only sound evidence that we are true children of God.* Children in this world are generally like their parents. Some, doubtless, are more so, and some less—but it is seldom indeed that you cannot trace a kind of family likeness. And it is much the same with the children of God. The Lord Jesus says, "If ye were Abraham's children, ye would do the works of Abraham." "If God were your Father, ye would love me" (John 8:39, 42). If men have no likeness to the Father in heaven, it is vain to talk of their being His "sons." If we know nothing of holiness we may flatter ourselves as we please, but we have not got the Holy Spirit dwelling in us: we are dead, and must be brought to life again—we are lost, and must be found. "As many as are led by the Spirit of God, they," and they only, "are the sons of God" (Rom. 8:14). We must show by our lives the family we belong to. We must let men see by our good conversation that we are indeed the children of the Holy One, or our sonship is but an empty name. "Say not," says Gurnall, "that thou hast royal blood in thy veins, and art born of God, except thou canst prove thy pedigree by daring to be holy."

(f) We must be holy, because *this is the most likely way to do good to others.* We cannot live to ourselves only in this world. Our lives will always be doing either good or harm to those who see them. They are a silent sermon, which all can read. It is sad indeed when they are a sermon for the devil's cause, and not for God's. I believe that far more is done for Christ's kingdom by the holy living of believers than we are at all aware of. There is a reality about such living that makes men feel, and obliges them to think. It carries a weight and influence with it that nothing else can give. It makes religion beautiful, and draws men to consider it, like a lighthouse seen afar off. The day of judgment will prove that many besides husbands have been won "without the word" by a holy life (1 Pet. 3:1). You may talk to persons about the doctrines of the Gospels, and few will listen, and still fewer understand. But your life is an argument that none can escape. There is a meaning about holiness that not even the most unlearned can help taking in. They may not understand justification, but they can understand love. I believe there is far more harm done by unholy and inconsistent Christians than we are aware of. Such men are among Satan's best allies. They pull down by their lives what ministers build with their lips. They cause the chariot wheels of the gospel to drive heavily. They supply the children of this world with a never-ending excuse for remaining as they are. "I cannot see the use of so much religion," said an irreligious tradesman not long ago; "I observe that some of my customers are always talking about the gospel, and faith, and election, and the blessed promises, and so forth; and yet these very people think nothing of cheating me of pence and half-pence, when they have an opportunity. Now, if religious persons can do such things,

I do not see what good there is in religion." I grieve to be obliged to write such things, but I fear that Christ's name is too often blasphemed because of the lives of Christians. Let us take heed lest the blood of souls should be required at our hands. From murder of souls by inconsistency and loose walking, good Lord, deliver us! Oh, for the sake of others, if for no other reason, let us strive to be holy!

(g) We must be holy, because *our present comfort depends much upon it.* We cannot be too often reminded of this. We are sadly apt to forget that there is a close connection between sin and sorrow, holiness and happiness, sanctification and consolation. God has so wisely ordered it, that our well-being and our well-doing are linked together. He has mercifully provided that even in this world it shall be man's interest to be holy. Our justification is not by works—our calling and election are not according to our works—but it is vain for anyone to suppose that he will have a lively sense of his justification, or an assurance of his calling, so long as he neglects good works, or does not strive to live a holy life. "Hereby we do know that we know him, if we keep his commandments." "Hereby we know that we are of the truth, and shall assure our hearts" (1 John 2:3; 3:19). A believer may as soon expect to feel the sun's rays upon a dark and cloudy day, as to feel strong consolation in Christ while he does not follow Him fully. When the disciples forsook the Lord and fled, they escaped danger, but they were miserable and sad. When, shortly after, they confessed Him boldly before men, they were cast into prison and beaten; but we are told "they rejoiced that they were counted worthy to suffer shame for his name" (Acts 5:41). Oh, for our own sakes, if there were no other reason, let us strive to be holy! He who follows Jesus most fully will always follow Him most comfortably.

(h) Lastly, we must be holy, because *without holiness on earth we shall never be prepared to enjoy heaven.* Heaven is a holy place. The Lord of heaven is a holy Being. The angels are holy creatures. Holiness is written on everything in heaven. The book of Revelation says expressly, "There shall in no wise enter into it anything that defileth, neither whatsoever worketh abomination, or maketh a lie" (Rev. 21:27).

I appeal solemnly to everyone who reads these pages, How shall we ever be at home and happy in heaven, if we die unholy? Death works no change. The grave makes no alteration. Each will rise again with the same character in which he breathed his last. Where will our place be if we are strangers to holiness now?

Suppose for a moment that you were allowed to enter heaven without holiness. What would you do? What possible enjoyment could you feel there? To which of all the saints would you join yourself, and by whose side would you sit down? Their pleasures are not your pleasures, their tastes not your tastes, their character not your character. How could you possibly be happy, if you had not been holy on earth?

Now perhaps you love the company of the light and the careless, the worldly minded and the covetous, the reveler and the pleasure-seeker, the ungodly and the profane. There will be none such in heaven.

Now perhaps you think the saints of God too strict and particular, and serious. You rather avoid them. You have no delight in their society. There will be no other company in heaven.

Now perhaps you think praying, and Scripture reading, and hymn singing, dull and melancholy, and stupid work—a thing to be tolerated now and then, but not enjoyed. You reckon the Sabbath a burden and a weariness; you could not possibly spend more than a small part of it in worshiping God. But remember, heaven is a never-ending Sabbath. The inhabitants thereof rest not day or night, saying, "Holy, holy, holy, Lord God Almighty" and singing the praise of the Lamb. How could an unholy man find pleasure in occupation such as this?

Think you that such a one would delight to meet David, and Paul, and John, after a life spent in doing the very things they spoke against? Would he take sweet counsel with them, and find that he and they had much in common? Think you, above all, that he would rejoice to meet Jesus, the Crucified One, face to face, after cleaving to the sins for which He died, after loving His enemies and despising His friends? Would he stand before Him with confidence, and join in the cry, "This is our God; we have waited for him, we will be glad and rejoice in his salvation"? (Isa. 25:9). Think you not rather that the tongue of an unholy man would cleave to the roof of his mouth with shame, and his only desire would be to be cast out! He would feel a stranger in a land he knew not, a black sheep amidst Christ's holy flock. The voice of cherubim and seraphim, the song of angels and archangels and all the company of heaven, would be a language he could not understand. The very air would seem an air he could not breathe.

I know not what others may think, but to me it does seem clear that heaven would be a miserable place to an unholy man. It cannot be otherwise. People may say, in a vague way, they "hope to go to heaven"; but they do not consider what they say. There must be a certain "meetness for the inheritance of the saints in light." Our hearts must be somewhat in tune. To reach the holiday of glory, we must pass through the training school of grace. We must be heavenly minded, and have heavenly tastes, in the life that now is, or else we shall never find ourselves in heaven, in the life to come.

And now, before I go any further, let me say a few words by way of application.

(1) For one thing, let me ask everyone who may read these pages, *Are you holy?* Listen, I pray you, to the question I put to you this day. Do you know anything of the holiness of which I have been speaking?

I do not ask whether you attend your church regularly—whether you have been baptized, and received the Lord's Supper—whether you have the name of Christian—I ask something more than all this: *Are you holy, or are you not?*

I do not ask whether you approve of holiness in others—whether you like to read the lives of holy people, and to talk of holy things, and to have on your table holy books—whether you mean to be holy, and hope you will be holy someday—I ask something further: *Are you yourself holy this very day, or are you not?*

And why do I ask so straitly, and press the question so strongly? I do it because the Scripture says, *"Without holiness no man shall see the Lord."* It is written, it is not my fancy—it is the Bible, not my private opinion—it is the word of God, not of man—"Without holiness no man shall see the Lord" (Heb. 12:14).

Alas, what searching, sifting words are these! What thoughts come across my mind, as I write them down! I look at the world, and see the greater part of it lying in wickedness. I look at professing Christians, and see the vast majority having nothing of Christianity but the name. I turn to the Bible, and I hear the Spirit saying, "Without holiness no man shall see the Lord."

Surely it is a text that ought to make us consider our ways, and search our hearts. Surely it should raise within us solemn thoughts, and send us to prayer.

You may try to put me off by saying you "feel much, and think much about these things: far more than many suppose." I answer, "This is not the point. The poor lost souls in hell do as much as this. The great question is not what you think, and what you feel, but what you do."

You may say, "It was never meant that all Christians should be holy, and that holiness," such as I have described, "is only for great saints, and people of uncommon gifts." I answer, "I cannot see that in Scripture. I read that every man who hath hope in

Christ purifieth himself" (1 John 3:3). "Without holiness no man shall see the Lord."

You may say, "It is impossible to be so holy and to do our duty in this life at the same time; the thing cannot be done." I answer, "You are mistaken. *It can be done.* With Christ on your side nothing is impossible. It *has* been done by many. David, and Obadiah, and Daniel, and the servants of Nero's household, are all examples that go to prove it."

You may say, "If I were so holy I would be unlike other people." I answer, "I know it well. It is just what you ought to be. Christ's true servants always were unlike the world around them —a separate nation, a peculiar people; and you must be so too, if you would be saved!"

You may say, "At this rate very few will be saved." I answer, "I know it. It is precisely what we are told in the Sermon on the Mount." The Lord Jesus said so 2,000 years ago. "Strait is the gate, and narrow is the way, that leadeth unto life, and few there be that find it" (Matt. 7:14). Few will be saved, because few will take the trouble to seek salvation. Men will not deny themselves the pleasures of sin and their own way for a little season. They turn their backs on an "inheritance incorruptible, undefiled, and that fadeth not away." "Ye will not come unto me," says Jesus, "that ye might have life" (John 5:40).

You may say, "These are hard sayings: the way is very narrow." I answer, "I know it. So says the Sermon on the Mount." The Lord Jesus said so 2,000 years ago. He always said that men must take up the cross daily, and that they must be ready to cut off hand or foot, if they would be His disciples. It is in religion as it is in other things, "there are no gains without pains." That which costs nothing is worth nothing.

Whatever we may think fit to say, we must be holy, if we would see the Lord. Where is our Christianity if we are not? We must not merely have a Christian name, and Christian knowledge, we must have a Christian character also. We must be saints on earth, if ever we mean to be saints in heaven. God has said it, and He will not go back: "Without holiness no man shall see the Lord." "The Pope's calendar," says Jenkyn, "only makes saints of the dead, but Scripture requires sanctity in the living." "Let not men deceive themselves," says Owen; "sanctification is a qualification indispensably necessary unto those who will be under the conduct of the Lord Christ unto salvation. He leads none to heaven but whom he sanctifies on the earth. This living Head will not admit of dead members."

Surely we need not wonder that Scripture says, "Ye must be born again" (John 3:7). Surely it is clear as noonday that many professing Christians need a complete change—new hearts, new natures—if ever they are to be saved. Old things must pass away; they must become new creatures. "Without holiness no man," be he who he may, "shall see the Lord."

(2) Let me, for another thing, speak a little to believers. I ask you this question, *Do you think you feel the importance of holiness as much as you should?*

I own I fear the temper of the times about this subject. I doubt exceedingly whether it holds that place it deserves in the thoughts and attention of some of the Lord's people. I would humbly suggest that we are apt to overlook the doctrine of growth in grace, and that we do not sufficiently consider how very far a person may go in a profession of religion, and yet have no grace, and be dead in God's sight after all. I believe that Judas Iscariot seemed very like the other apostles. When the Lord warned them that one would betray Him, no one said, "Is it Judas?" We had better think more about the churches of Sardis and Laodicea than we do.

I have no desire to make an idol of holiness. I do not wish to dethrone Christ and put holiness in His place. But I must candidly say, I wish sanctification was more thought of in this day than it seems to be, and I therefore take occasion to press the subject on all believers into whose hands these pages may fall. I fear it is sometimes forgotten that God has married together justification and sanctification. They are distinct and different things, beyond question, but one is never found without the other. All justified people are sanctified, and all sanctified are justified. What God has joined together let no man dare to put asunder. Tell me not of your justification, unless you have also some marks of sanctification. Boast not of Christ's work for you, unless you can show us the Spirit's work in you. Think not that Christ and the Spirit can ever be divided. I doubt not that many believers know these things, but I think it good for us to be put in remembrance of them. Let us prove that we know them by our lives. Let us try to keep in view this text more continually: "Follow holiness, without which no man shall see the Lord."

I must frankly say I wish there was not such an excessive sensitiveness on the subject of holiness as I sometimes perceive in the minds of believers. A man might really think it was a dangerous subject to handle, so cautiously is it touched! Yet surely when we have exalted Christ as "the way, the truth, and the life," we cannot err in speaking strongly about what should be the character of His people. Well says Rutherford, "The way that crieth down duties and sanctification, is not the way of grace. Believing and doing are blood-friends."

I would say it with all reverence, but say it I must—I sometimes fear if Christ were on earth now, there are not a few who would think His preaching legal; and if Paul were writing his Epistles, there are those who would think he had better not write the latter part of most of them as he did. But let us remember that the Lord Jesus did speak the Sermon on the Mount, and that the Epistle to the Ephesians contains six chapters and not four. I grieve to feel obliged to speak in this way, but I am sure there is a cause.

That great divine, John Owen, the dean of Christ Church, used to say, more than two hundred years ago, that there were people whose whole religion seemed to consist in going about complaining of their own corruptions, and telling everyone that they could do nothing of themselves. I am afraid that after two centuries the same thing might be said with truth of some of Christ's professing people in this day. I know there are texts in Scripture that warrant such complaints. I do not object to them when they come from men who walk in the steps of the Apostle Paul, and fight a good fight, as he did, against sin, the devil, and the world. But I never like such complaints when I see ground for suspecting, as I often do, that they are only a cloak to cover spiritual laziness, and an excuse for spiritual sloth. If we say with Paul, "O wretched man that I am," let us also be able to say with him, "I press toward the mark." Let us not quote his example in one thing, while we do not follow him in another (Rom. 7:24; Phil. 3:14).

I do not set up myself to be better than other people, and if anyone asks, "What are you, that you write in this way?" I answer, "I am a very poor creature indeed." But I say that I cannot read the Bible without desiring to see many believers more spiritual, more holy, more single-eyed, more heavenly minded, more wholehearted than they are today. I want to see among believers more of a pilgrim spirit, a more decided separation from the world, a conversation more evidently in heaven, a closer walk with God—and therefore I have written as I have.

Is it not true that we need a higher standard of personal holiness in this day? Where is our patience? Where is our zeal? Where is our love? Where are our works? Where is the power of religion to be seen, as it was in times gone by? Where is that unmistakable tone that used to distinguish the saints of old, and shake the world? Verily our silver has become dross, our wine mixed with water, and our salt has very little savor. We are all more than half asleep. The night is far spent, and the day is at hand. Let us awake, and sleep no more. Let us open our eyes more widely than we have done hitherto. "Let us lay aside every weight, and the sin that doth so easily beset us." "Let us cleanse ourselves from all filthiness of flesh and spirit, and perfect holiness in the fear of God" (Heb. 12:1; 2 Cor. 7:1). "Did Christ die," says Owen, "and shall sin live? Was he crucified in the world, and shall our affections to the world be quick and lively? Oh, where is the spirit of him, who by the cross of Christ was crucified to the world, and the world to him!"

III. Let me, in the last place, offer a *word of advice to all who desire to be holy.*

Would you be holy? Would you become a new creature? Then you must *begin with Christ.* You will do just nothing at all, and make no progress till you feel your sin and weakness, and flee to Him. He is the root and beginning of all holiness, and the way to be holy is to come to Him by faith and be joined to Him. Christ is not wisdom and righteousness only to His people, but sanctification also. Men sometimes try to make themselves holy first of all, and sad work they make of it. They toil and labor, and turn over new leaves, and make many changes; and yet, like the woman with the issue of blood, before she came to Christ, they feel "nothing bettered, but rather worse" (Mark 5:26). They run in vain, and labor in vain; and little wonder, for they are beginning at the wrong end. They are building up a wall of sand; their work runs down as fast as they throw it up. They are bailing water out of a leaky vessel: the leak gains on them, not they on the leak. Other foundation of "holiness" can no man lay than that which Paul laid, even Christ Jesus. "Without Christ we can do nothing" (John 15:5). It is a strong but true saying of Traill's, "Wisdom out of Christ is damning folly—righteousness out of Christ is guilt and condemnation—sanctification out of Christ is filth and sin—redemption out of Christ is bondage and slavery."

Do you want to attain holiness? Do you feel this day a real hearty desire to be holy? Would you be a partaker of the divine nature? Then *go to Christ.* Wait for nothing. Wait for nobody. Linger not. Think not to make yourself ready. Go and say to Him, in the words of that beautiful hymn—

> Nothing in my hand I bring,
> Simply to thy cross I cling;
> Naked, flee to thee for dress;
> Helpless, look to thee for grace.[1]

There is not a brick nor a stone laid in the work of our sanctification till we go to Christ. Holiness is His special gift to His believing people. Holiness is the work He carries on in their hearts, by the Spirit whom He puts within them. He is appointed "a Prince and a Savior, to give repentance" as well as remission of sins. "To as many as receive him, he gives power to become sons of God" (Acts 5:31; John 1:12–13). Holiness comes not of blood—parents cannot give it to their children: nor yet of the will of the flesh—man cannot produce it in himself: nor yet of the will of man—ministers cannot give it you by baptism. Holiness comes from Christ. It is the result of vital union with Him. It is the fruit of being a living branch of the true Vine. Go then to Christ and say, "Lord, not only save me from the guilt of sin, but send the Spirit, whom You promised, and save me from its power. Make me holy. Teach me to do Your will."

Would you continue holy? Then *abide in Christ.* He says Himself, "Abide in me and I in you." "He that abideth in me and I in him, the same beareth much fruit" (John 15:4–5). It pleased the Father that in Him should all fullness dwell—a full supply for all a believer's wants. He is the Physician to whom you must daily go, if you would keep well. He is the Manna that you must daily eat, and the Rock of which you must daily drink. His arm is the arm on which you must daily lean, as you come up out of the wilderness of this world. You must not only be rooted, you must also be built up in Him. Paul was a man of God indeed—a holy man—a growing, thriving Christian—and what was the secret of it all? He was one to whom Christ was "all in all." He was ever "looking unto Jesus." "I can do all things," he says, "through Christ which strengtheneth me." "I live, yet not I, but Christ liveth in me. The life that I now live, I live by the faith of the Son of God" (Heb. 12:2; Phil. 4:13; Gal. 2:20). Let us go and do likewise.

May all who read these pages know these things by experience, and not by hearsay only. May we all feel the importance of holiness, far more than we have ever done yet! May our years be holy years with our souls, and then they will be happy ones! Whether we live, may we live unto the Lord; or whether we die, may we die unto the Lord; or if He comes for us, may we be found in peace, without spot, and blameless!

1. Editor's note: from "Rock of Ages" by Augustus M. Toplady.

4

The Fight

∞

"FIGHT THE GOOD FIGHT OF FAITH." *(1 Timothy 6:12)*

IT IS A CURIOUS FACT that there is no subject about which most people feel such deep interest as "fighting." Young men and maidens, old men and little children, high and low, rich and poor, learned and unlearned, all feel a deep interest in wars, battles, and fighting.

This is a simple fact, whatever way we may try to explain it. We should call that Englishman a dull fellow who cared nothing about the story of Waterloo, or Inkermann, or Balaclava, or Lucknow. We should think that heart cold and stupid which was not moved and thrilled by the struggles at Sedan, and Strasburg, and Metz, and Paris, during the war between France and Germany.

But there is another warfare of far greater importance than any war that was ever waged by man. It is a warfare that concerns not two or three nations only, but every Christian man and woman born into the world. The warfare I speak of is the spiritual warfare.

It is the fight that everyone who would be saved must fight about his soul.

This warfare, I am aware, is a thing of which many know nothing. Talk to them about it, and they are ready to set you down as a madman, an enthusiast, or a fool. And yet it is as real and true as any war the world has ever seen. It has its hand-to-hand conflicts and its wounds. It has its watchings and fatigues. It has its sieges and assaults. It has its victories and its defeats. Above all, it has consequences, which are awful, tremendous, and most peculiar. In earthly warfare the consequences to nations are often temporary and remediable. In the spiritual warfare it is very different. Of that warfare, the consequences, when the fight is over, are unchangeable and eternal.

It is of this warfare that St. Paul spoke to Timothy, when he wrote those burning words, "Fight the good fight of faith; lay hold on eternal life." It is of this warfare that I propose to speak in this chapter. I hold the subject to be closely connected with that of sanctification and holiness. He who would understand the nature of true holiness must know that the Christian is "a man of war." If we would be holy we must fight.

I. The first thing I have to say is this: *True Christianity is a fight.*

True Christianity! Let us mind that word "true." There is a vast quantity of religion current in the world that is not true, genuine Christianity. It passes muster; it satisfies sleepy consciences; but it is not good money. It is not the real thing that was called Christianity 1,800 years ago. There are thousands of men and women who go to churches and chapels every Sunday, and call themselves Christians. Their names are in the baptismal register. They are reckoned Christians while they live. They are married with a Christian marriage service. They mean to be buried as Christians when they die. But you never see any "fight" about their religion! Of spiritual strife, and exertion, and conflict, and self-denial, and watching, and warring, they know literally nothing at all. Such Christianity may satisfy man, and those who say anything against it may be thought very hard and uncharitable; but it certainly is not the Christianity of the Bible. It is not the religion that the Lord Jesus founded, and His apostles preached. It is not the religion that produces real holiness. True Christianity is "a fight."

The true Christian is called to be a soldier, and must behave as such from the day of his conversion to the day of his death. He is not meant to live a life of religious ease, indolence, and security. He must never imagine for a moment that he can sleep and doze along the way to heaven, like one traveling in an easy carriage. If he takes his standard of Christianity from the children of this world, he may be content with such notions; but he will find no countenance for them in the Word of God. If the Bible is the rule of his faith and practice, he will find his course laid down very plainly in this matter. He must "fight."

With whom is the Christian soldier meant to fight? Not with other Christians. Wretched indeed is that man's idea of religion who fancies that it consists in perpetual controversy! He who is never satisfied unless he is engaged in some strife between church and church, chapel and chapel, sect and sect, faction and faction, party and party, knows nothing yet as he ought to know. No doubt it may be absolutely needful sometimes to appeal to law courts, in order to ascertain the right interpretation of a church's articles, and rubrics, and formularies. But, as a general rule, the cause of sin is never so much helped as when Christians waste their strength in quarreling with one another, and spend their time in petty squabbles.

No, indeed! The principal fight of the Christian is with the world, the flesh, and the devil. These are his never-dying foes. These are the three chief enemies against whom he must wage war. Unless he gets the victory over these three, all other victories are useless and vain. If he had a nature like an angel, and were not a fallen creature, the warfare would not be so essential. But with a corrupt heart, a busy devil, and an ensnaring world, he must either "fight" or be lost.

He must fight *the flesh*. Even after conversion he carries within him a nature prone to evil, and a heart weak and unstable as water. That heart will never be free from imperfection in this world, and it is a miserable delusion to expect it. To keep that heart from going astray, the Lord Jesus bids us "watch and pray." The spirit may be ready, but the flesh is weak. There is need of a daily struggle and a daily wrestling in prayer. "I keep under my body," cries St. Paul, "and bring it into subjection." "I see a law in my members warring against the law of my mind, and bringing me into captivity." "O wretched man that I am, who shall deliver me from the body of this death?" "They that are Christ's have crucified the flesh with the affections and lusts." "Mortify your members which are upon the earth" (Mark 14:38; 1 Cor. 9:27; Rom. 7:23–24; Gal. 5:24; Col. 3:5).

He must fight *the world.* The subtle influence of that mighty enemy must be daily resisted, and without a daily battle can never be overcome. The love of the world's good things—the fear of the world's laughter or blame—the secret desire to keep in with the world—the secret wish to do as others in the world do, and not to run into extremes—all these are spiritual foes, which beset the Christian continually on his way to heaven, and must be conquered. "The friendship of the world is enmity with God: whosoever therefore will be a friend of the world is the enemy of God." "If any man love the world, the love of the Father is not in him." "The world is crucified to me, and I unto the world." "Whatsoever is born of God overcometh the world." "Be not conformed to this world" (James 4:4; 1 John 2:15; Gal. 6:14; 1 John 5:4; Rom. 12:2).

He must fight *the devil.* That old enemy of mankind is not dead. Ever since the fall of Adam and Eve, he has been "going to and fro in the earth, and walking up and down in it," and striving to compass one great end—the ruin of man's soul. Never slumbering and never sleeping, he is always "going about as a lion seeking whom he may devour." An unseen enemy, he is always near us, about our path and about our bed, and spying out all our ways. "A murderer" and "a liar" from the beginning, he labors night and day to cast us down to hell. Sometimes by leading into superstition, sometimes by suggesting doubt, sometimes by one kind of tactics and sometimes by another, he is always carrying on a campaign against our souls. "Satan hath desired to have you, that he may sift you as wheat." This mighty adversary must be daily resisted if we wish to be saved. But "this kind goeth not out" but by watching and praying, and fighting, and putting on the whole armor of God. The strong man armed will never be kept out of our hearts without a daily battle (Job 1:7; 1 Pet. 5:8; John 8:44; Luke 22:31; [Matt. 17:21]; Eph. 6:11).

Some men may think these statements too strong. You fancy that I am going too far, and laying on the colors too thickly. You are secretly saying to yourself, that men and women in England may surely get to heaven without all this trouble and warfare and fighting. Listen to me for a few minutes, and I will show you that I have something to say on God's behalf.

Remember the maxim of the wisest general that ever lived in England—"In time of war it is the worst mistake to underrate your enemy, and try to make a little war." This Christian warfare is no light matter. Give me your attention and consider what I say. What says the Scripture?—"Fight the good fight of faith. Lay hold on eternal life." "Endure hardness as a good soldier of Jesus Christ." "Put on the whole armor of God, that ye may be able to stand against the wiles of the devil. For we wrestle not against flesh and blood, but against principalities, against powers, against the ruler of the darkness of this world, against spiritual wickedness in high places. Wherefore take unto you the whole armor of God, that you may be able to withstand in the evil day, and having done all to stand." "Strive to enter in at the strait gate." "Labor for the meat that endureth unto everlasting life." "Think not that I came to send peace on the earth: I came not to send peace but a sword." "He that hath no sword let him sell his garment and buy one." "Watch ye, stand fast in the faith, quit you like men, be strong." "War a good warfare, holding faith and a good conscience" (1 Tim. 6:12; 2 Tim. 2:3; Eph. 6:11–13; Luke 13:24; John 6:27; Matt. 10:34; Luke 22:36; 1 Cor. 16:13; 1 Tim. 1:18–19). Words such as these appear to me clear, plain, and unmistakable. They all teach one and the same great lesson, if we are willing to receive it. That lesson is, that true Christianity is a struggle, a fight, and a warfare. He who pretends to condemn "fighting" and teaches that we ought to sit still and "yield ourselves to God," appears to me to misunderstand his Bible, and to make a great mistake.

What says the Baptismal Service of the Church of England? No doubt that service is uninspired, and, like every uninspired composition, it has its defects; but to the millions of people all over the globe, who profess and call themselves English churchmen, its voice ought to speak with some weight. And what does it say? It tells us that over every new member who is admitted into the Church of England the following words are used—

I baptize thee in the name of the Father, the Son, and the Holy Ghost. . . . I sign this child with the sign of the cross, in token that hereafter he shall not be ashamed to confess the faith of Christ crucified, and manfully to fight under His banner against sin, the world, and the devil, and to continue Christ's faithful soldier and servant unto his life's end.

Of course we all know that in myriads of cases baptism is a mere form, and that parents bring their children to the font without faith or prayer or thought, and consequently receive no blessing. The man who supposes that baptism in such cases acts mechanically, like a medicine, and that godly and ungodly, praying and prayerless parents, all alike get the same benefit for their children, must be in a strange state of mind. But one thing, at any rate, is very certain. Every baptized churchman is by his profession a "soldier of Jesus Christ," and is pledged "to fight under his banner against sin, the world, and the devil." He that doubts it had better take up his Prayer Book, and read, mark, and learn its contents. The worst thing about many very zealous churchmen is their total ignorance of what their own Prayer Book contains.

Whether we are churchmen or not, one thing is certain—this Christian warfare is a great reality, and a subject of vast importance. It is not a matter like church government and ceremonial, about which men may differ, and yet reach heaven at last. Necessity is laid upon us. We must fight. There are no promises in the Lord Jesus Christ's epistles to the seven churches [in

Revelation], except to those who "overcome." Where there is grace, there will be conflict. The believer is a soldier. There is no holiness without a warfare. Saved souls will always be found to have fought a fight.

It is a fight of *absolute necessity*. Let us not think that in this war we can remain neutral and sit still. Such a line of action may be possible in the strife of nations, but it is utterly impossible in that conflict that concerns the soul. The boasted policy of noninterference—the "masterly inactivity" that pleases so many statesmen—the plan of keeping quiet and letting things alone—all this will never do in the Christian warfare. Here at any rate no one can escape serving under the plea that he is "a man of peace." To be at peace with the world, the flesh, and the devil, is to be at enmity with God, and in the broad way that leads to destruction. We have no choice or option. We must either fight or be lost.

It is a fight of *universal necessity*. No rank, or class, or age, can plead exemption, or escape the battle. Ministers and people, preachers and hearers, old and young, high and low, rich and poor, gentle and simple, kings and subjects, landlords and tenants, learned and unlearned—all alike must carry arms and go to war. All have by nature a heart full of pride, unbelief, sloth, worldliness, and sin. All are living in a world beset with snares, traps, and pitfalls for the soul. All have near them a busy, restless, malicious devil. All, from the queen in her palace down to the pauper in the workhouse, all must fight, if they would be saved.

It is a fight of *perpetual necessity*. It admits of no breathing time, no armistice, no truce. On weekdays as well as on Sundays —in private as well as in public—at home by the family fireside as well as abroad—in little things like management of tongue and temper, as well as in great ones like the government of kingdoms—the Christian's warfare must unceasingly go on. The foe we have to do with keeps no holidays, never slumbers, and never sleeps. So long as we have breath in our bodies, we must keep on our armor, and remember we are on an enemy's ground. "Even on the brink of Jordan," said a dying saint, "I find Satan nibbling at my heels." We must fight till we die.

Let us consider well these propositions. Let us take care that our own personal religion is real, genuine, and true. The saddest symptom about many so-called Christians is the utter absence of anything like conflict and fight in their Christianity. They eat, they drink, they dress, they work, they amuse themselves, they get money, they spend money, they go through a scanty round of formal religious services once or twice every week. But the great spiritual warfare—its watchings and strugglings, its agonies and anxieties, its battles and contests—of all this they appear to know nothing at all. Let us take care that this case is not our own. The worst state of soul is "when the strong man armed keepeth the house, and his goods are at peace"—when he leads men and women "captive at his will," and they make no resistance. The worst chains are those that are neither felt nor seen by the prisoner (Luke 11:21; 2 Tim. 2:26).

We may take comfort about our souls if we know anything

of an inward fight and conflict. It is the invariable companion of genuine Christian holiness. It is not everything, I am well aware, but it is something. Do we find in our heart of hearts a spiritual struggle? Do we feel anything of the flesh lusting against the spirit and the spirit against the flesh, so that we cannot do the things we would? (Gal. 5:17). Are we conscious of two principles within us, contending for the mastery? Do we feel anything of war in our inward man? Well, let us thank God for it! It is a good sign. It is strongly probable evidence of the great work of sanctification. All true saints are soldiers. Anything is better than apathy, stagnation, deadness, and indifference. We are in a better state than many. The most part of so-called Christians have no feeling at all. We are evidently no friends of Satan. Like the kings of this world, he wars not against his own subjects. The very fact that he assaults us should fill our minds with hope. I say again, let us take comfort. The child of God has two great marks about him, and of these two we have one. He may be known by his inward warfare, as well as by his inward peace.

II. I pass on to the second thing that I have to say in handling my subject: *True Christianity is the fight of faith.*

In this respect the Christian warfare is utterly unlike the conflicts of this world. It does not depend on the strong arm, the quick eye, or the swift foot. It is not waged with carnal weapons, but with spiritual. Faith is the hinge on which victory turns. Success depends entirely on believing.

A general faith in the truth of God's written Word is the

primary foundation of the Christian soldier's character. He is what he is, does what he does, thinks as he thinks, acts as he acts, hopes as he hopes, behaves as he behaves, for one simple reason—he believes certain propositions revealed and laid down in Holy Scripture. "He that cometh to God must believe that he is, and that he is a rewarder of them that diligently seek him" (Heb. 11:6).

A religion without doctrine or dogma is a thing that many are fond of talking of in the present day. It sounds very fine at first. It looks very pretty at a distance. But the moment we sit down to examine and consider it, we shall find it a simple impossibility. We might as well talk of a body without bones and sinews. No man will ever be anything or do anything in religion, unless he believes something. Even those who profess to hold the miserable and uncomfortable views of the deists are obliged to confess that they believe *something*. With all their bitter sneers against dogmatic theology and Christian credulity, as they call it, they themselves have a kind of faith.

As for true Christians, faith is the very backbone of their spiritual existence. No one ever fights earnestly against the world, the flesh, and the devil, unless he has engraven on his heart certain great principles that he believes. What they are he may hardly know, and may certainly not be able to define or write down. But there they are, and, consciously or unconsciously, they form the roots of his religion. Wherever you see a man, whether rich or poor, learned or unlearned, wrestling manfully with sin, and trying to overcome it, you may be sure there are certain great princi-

ples which that man believes. The poet who wrote the famous
lines,

> For modes of faith let graceless zealots fight,
> He can't be wrong whose life is in the right,[1]

was a clever man, but a poor divine. There is no such thing as
right living without faith and believing.

*A special faith in our Lord Jesus Christ's person, work, and
office* is the life, heart, and mainspring of the Christian soldier's
character.

He sees by faith an unseen Savior, who loved him, gave
Himself for him, paid his debts for him, bore his sins, carried his
transgressions, rose again for him, and appears in heaven for him
as his Advocate at the right hand of God. He sees Jesus and clings
to Him. Seeing this Savior and trusting in Him, he feels peace and
hope, and willingly does battle against the foes of his soul.

He sees his own many sins—his weak heart, a tempting
world, a busy devil; and if he looked only at them he might well
despair. But he sees also a mighty Savior, an interceding Savior, a
sympathizing Savior—His blood, His righteousness, His everlasting priesthood—and he believes that all this is his own. He sees
Jesus and casts his whole weight on Him. Seeing Him, he cheer-
fully fights on, with a full confidence that he will prove "more
than conqueror through him that loved him" (Rom. 8:37).

Habitual lively faith in Christ's presence and readiness to help is the secret of the Christian soldier fighting successfully.

It must never be forgotten that faith admits of degrees. All men do not believe alike, and even the same person has his ebbs and flows of faith, and believes more heartily at one time than another. According to the degree of his faith, the Christian fights well or ill, wins victories, or suffers occasional repulses, comes off triumphant, or loses a battle. He who has most faith will always be the happiest and most comfortable soldier. Nothing makes the anxieties of warfare sit so lightly on a man as the assurance of Christ's love and continual protection. Nothing enables him to bear the fatigue of watching, struggling, and wrestling against sin like the indwelling confidence that Christ is on his side and success is sure. It is the "shield of faith" that quenches all the fiery darts of the wicked one. It is the man who can say, "I know whom I have believed"—who can say in time of suffering, "I am not ashamed." He who wrote those glowing words, "We faint not"; "Our light affliction which endureth but for a moment worketh in us a far more exceeding and eternal weight of glory" —was the man who wrote with the same pen, "We look not at the things which are seen, but at the things which are not seen; for the things which are seen are temporal, but the things which are not seen are eternal." It is the man who said, "I live by the faith of the Son of God," who said, in the same Epistle, "the world is crucified unto me, and I unto the world." It is the man who said, "To me to live is Christ," who said, in the same Epistle, "I have learned in whatsoever state I am therewith to be content"; "I can do all things through Christ." The more faith, the more victory! The more faith, the more inward peace! (Eph. 6:16; 2 Tim. 1:12; 2 Cor. 4:16–18; Gal. 2:20; 6:14; Phil. 1:21; 4:11, 13).

I think it impossible to overrate the value and importance of faith. Well may the Apostle Peter call it "precious" (2 Pet. 1:1). Time would fail me if I tried to recount a hundredth part of the victories that by faith Christian soldiers have obtained.

Let us take down our Bibles and read with attention the eleventh chapter of the Epistle to the Hebrews. Let us mark the long list of worthies whose names are thus recorded, from Abel down to Moses, even before Christ was born of the Virgin Mary, and brought life and immortality into full light by the gospel. Let us note well what battles they won against the world, the flesh, and the devil. And then let us remember that believing did it all. These men looked forward to the promised Messiah. They saw Him who is invisible. "By faith the elders obtained a good report" (Heb. 11:2–27).

Let us turn to the pages of early church history. Let us see how the primitive Christians held fast their religion even unto death, and were not shaken by the fiercest persecutions of heathen emperors. For centuries there were never wanting men like Polycarp and Ignatius, who were ready to die rather than deny Christ. Fines, and prisons, and torture, and fire, and sword, were unable to crush the spirit of the noble army of martyrs. The whole power of imperial Rome, the mistress of the world, proved unable to stamp out the religion that began with a few fishermen and publicans in Palestine! And then let us remember that *believing* in an unseen Jesus was the church's strength. They won their victory by faith.

Let us examine the story of the Protestant Reformation. Let us study the lives of its leading champions—Wycliffe, and Huss, and Luther, and Ridley, and Latimer, and Hooper. Let us mark how these gallant soldiers of Christ stood firm against a host of adversaries, and were ready to die for their principles. What battles they fought! What controversies they maintained! What contradiction they endured! What tenacity of purpose they exhibited against a world in arms! And then let us remember that *believing* in an unseen Jesus was the secret of their strength. They overcame by faith.

Let us consider the men who have made the greatest marks in church history in the last hundred years. Let us observe how men like Wesley, and Whitefield, and Venn, and Romaine, stood alone in their day and generation, and revived English religion in the face of opposition from men high in office, and in the face of slander, ridicule, and persecution from nine-tenths of professing Christians in our land. Let us observe how men like William Wilberforce, and Havelock, and Hedley Vicars, have witnessed for Christ in the most difficult positions, and displayed a banner for Christ even at the regimental mess table, or on the floor of the House of Commons. Let us mark how these noble witnesses never flinched to the end, and won the respect even of their worst adversaries. And then let us remember that believing in an unseen Christ is the key to all their characters. By faith they lived, and walked, and stood, and overcame.

Would anyone live the life of a Christian soldier? Let him pray for faith. It is the gift of God; and a gift that those who ask shall never ask for in vain. You must believe before you do. If men do nothing in religion, it is because they do not believe. Faith is the first step toward heaven.

Would anyone fight the fight of a Christian soldier successfully and prosperously? Let him pray for a continual increase of faith. Let him abide in Christ, get closer to Christ, tighten his hold on Christ every day that he lives. Let his daily prayer be that of the disciples—"Lord, increase my faith" (Luke 17:5). Watch jealously over your faith, if you have any. It is the citadel of the Christian character, on which the safety of the whole fortress depends. It is the point that Satan loves to assail. All lies at his mercy if faith is overthrown. Here, if we love life, we must especially stand on our guard.

III. The last thing I have to say is this: *True Christianity is a good fight.*

"Good" is a curious word to apply to any warfare. All worldly war is more or less evil. No doubt it is an absolute necessity in many cases—to procure the liberty of nations, to prevent the weak from being trampled down by the strong—but still it is an evil. It entails an awful amount of bloodshed and suffering. It hurries into eternity myriads who are completely unprepared for their change. It calls forth the worst passions of man. It causes enormous waste and destruction of property. It fills peaceful homes with mourning widows and orphans. It spreads far and wide poverty, taxation, and national distress. It disarranges all the order of society. It interrupts the work of the gospel and the growth of Christian missions. In short, war is an immense and incalculable evil, and every praying man should cry night and day, "Give peace in our time." And yet there is one warfare that is emphatically "good," and one fight in which there is no evil. That warfare is the Christian warfare. That fight is the fight of the soul.

Now what are the reasons that the Christian fight is a "good fight"? What are the points in which his warfare is superior to the warfare of this world? Let me examine this matter, and open it out in order. I dare not pass the subject and leave it unnoticed. I want no one to begin the life of a Christian soldier without counting the cost. I would not keep back from anyone that if he would be holy and see the Lord he must fight, and that the Christian fight, though spiritual, is real and severe. It needs courage, boldness, and perseverance. But I want my readers to know that there is abundant encouragement, if they will only begin the battle. The Scripture does not call the Christian fight "a good fight" without reason and cause. Let me try to show what I mean.

(a) The Christian's fight is good, because *fought under the best of generals.* The Leader and Commander of all believers is our divine Savior, the Lord Jesus Christ—a Savior of perfect wisdom, infinite love, and almighty power. The Captain of our salvation never fails to lead His soldiers to victory. He never makes any useless movements, never errs in judgment, never commits any mistake. His eye is on all His followers, from the greatest of them even to the least. The humblest servant in His army is not forgotten. The weakest and most sickly is cared for, remembered, and kept unto salvation. The souls whom He has purchased and redeemed with His own blood are far too precious to be wasted and thrown away. Surely this is good!

(b) The Christian's fight is good, because *fought with the best of helps.* Weak as each believer is in himself, the Holy Spirit dwells in him, and his body is a temple of the Holy Ghost. Chosen by God the Father, washed in the blood of the Son, renewed by the Spirit, he does not go to warfare at his own charges, and is never alone. God the Holy Ghost daily teaches, leads, guides, and directs him. God the Father guards him by His almighty power. God the Son intercedes for him every moment, like Moses on the mount, while he is fighting in the valley below. A threefold cord like this can never be broken! His daily provisions and supplies never fail. His commissariat is never defective. His bread and his water are sure. Weak as he seems in himself, like a worm, he is strong in the Lord to do great exploits. Surely this is good!

(c) The Christian fight is a good fight, because *fought with the best of promises.* To every believer belong exceeding great and precious promises—all Yea and Amen in Christ—promises sure to be fulfilled, because made by One who cannot lie, and has power as well as will to keep His word. "Sin shall not have dominion over you." "The God of peace shall bruise Satan under your feet shortly." "He that has begun a good work will perform it until the day of Jesus Christ." "When thou passeth through the waters I will be with thee, and through the floods, they shall not overflow thee." "My sheep shall never perish, neither shall anyone pluck them out of my hand." "Him that cometh unto me I will in no wise cast out." "I will never leave thee, nor forsake thee." "I am persuaded that neither death, nor life, nor things present, nor things to come, shall be able to separate us from the love of God, which is in Christ Jesus" (Rom. 6:14; 16:20; Phil. 1:6; Isa. 43:2; John 10:28; 6:37; Heb. 13:5; Rom. 8:38). Words like these are worth their weight in gold! Who does not know that promises of coming aid have cheered the defenders of besieged cities, like Lucknow, and raised them above their natural strength? Have we never heard that the promise of "help before night" had much to say to the mighty victory of Waterloo? Yet all such promises are as nothing compared to the rich treasure of believers, the eternal promises of God. Surely this is good!

(d) The Christian's fight is a good fight, because *fought with the best of issues and results.* No doubt it is a war in which there are tremendous struggles, agonizing conflicts, wounds, bruises, watchings, fastings, and fatigue. But still every believer, without exception, is "more than conqueror through him that loved him" (Rom. 8:37). No soldiers of Christ are ever lost, missing, or left dead on the battlefield. No mourning will ever need to be put on, and no tears to be shed for either private or officer in the army of Christ. The muster roll, when the last evening comes, will be found precisely the same that it was in the morning. The English Guards marched out of London to the Crimean campaign a magnificent body of men; but many of the gallant fellows laid their bones in a foreign grave, and never saw London again. Far different shall be the arrival of the Christian army in "the city which hath foundations, whose builder and maker is God" (Heb. 11:10). Not one shall be found lacking. The words of our great Captain shall be found true: "Of them which thou hast given me I have lost none" (John 18:9). Surely this is good!

(e) The Christian's fight is good, because *it does good to the soul of him who fights it.* All other wars have a bad, lowering, and demoralizing tendency. They call forth the worst passions of the human mind. They harden the conscience, and sap the foundations of religion and morality. The Christian warfare alone tends to call forth the best things that are left in man. It promotes humility and charity, it lessens selfishness and worldliness, it induces men to set their affections on things above. The old, the sick, the dying, are never known to repent of fighting Christ's battles against sin, the world, and the devil. Their only regret is that they did not begin to serve Christ long before. The experience of that eminent saint, Philip Henry, does not stand alone. In his last days he said to his family, "I take you all to record that a life spent in the service of Christ is the happiest life that a man can spend upon earth." Surely this is good!

(f) The Christian's fight is a good fight, because *it does good to the world.* All other wars have a devastating, ravaging, and injurious effect. The march of an army through a land is an awful scourge to the inhabitants. Wherever it goes it impoverishes, wastes, and does harm. Injury to persons, property, feelings, and morals invariably accompanies it. Far different are the effects produced by Christian soldiers. Wherever they live they are a blessing. They raise the standard of religion and morality. They invariably check the progress of drunkenness, Sabbath breaking, profligacy, and dishonesty. Even their enemies are obliged to respect them. Go where you please, you will rarely find that barracks and garrisons do good to the neighborhood. But go where you please, you will find that the presence of a few true Christians is a blessing. Surely this is good!

(g) Finally, the Christian's fight is good, because *it ends in a glorious reward for all who fight it.* Who can tell the wages that Christ will pay to all His faithful people? Who can estimate the good things that our divine Captain has laid up for those who confess Him before men? A grateful country can give to her successful warriors medals, Victoria Crosses, pensions, peerages, honors, and titles. But it can give nothing that will last and endure forever, nothing that can be carried beyond the grave. Palaces like Blenheim and Strathfieldsay can only be enjoyed for a few years. The bravest generals and soldiers must go down one day before the king of terrors. Better, far better, is the position of him who fights under Christ's banner against sin, the world, and the devil. He may get little praise of man while he lives, and go down to the grave with little honor; but he shall have that which is far better, because far more enduring. He shall have "a crown of glory that fadeth not away" (1 Pet. 5:4). Surely this is good!

Let us settle it in our minds that the Christian fight is a good fight—really good, truly good, emphatically good. We see only part of it as yet. We see the struggle, but not the end; we see the campaign, but not the reward; we see the cross, but not the crown. We see a few humble, broken-spirited, penitent, praying people, enduring hardships and despised by the world; but we see not the hand of God over them, the face of God smiling on them, the kingdom of glory prepared for them. These things are yet to be revealed. Let us not judge by appearances. There are more good things about the Christian warfare than we see.

And now let me conclude my whole subject with a few words of practical application. Our lot is cast in times when the world seems thinking of little else but battles and fighting. The iron is entering into the soul of more than one nation, and the mirth of many a fair district is clean gone.

Surely in times like these a minister may fairly call on men to remember their spiritual warfare. Let me say a few parting words about the great fight of the soul.

(1) *It may be you are struggling hard for the rewards of this world.* Perhaps you are straining every nerve to obtain money, or

place, or power, or pleasure. If that be your case, take care. Your sowing will lead to a crop of bitter disappointment. Unless you mind what you are about, your latter end will be to lie down in sorrow.

Thousands have trodden the path you are pursuing, and have awoke too late to find it end in misery and eternal ruin. They have fought hard for wealth, and honor, and office, and promotion, and turned their backs on God, and Christ, and heaven, and the world to come. And what has their end been? Often, far too often, they have found out that their whole life has been a grand mistake. They have tasted by bitter experience the feelings of the dying statesman who cried aloud in his last hours, "The battle is fought: the battle is fought: but the victory is not won."

For your own happiness' sake, resolve this day to join the Lord's side. Shake off your past carelessness and unbelief. Come out from the ways of a thoughtless, unreasoning world. Take up the cross, and become a good soldier of Christ. "Fight the good fight of faith," that you may be happy as well as safe.

Think what the children of this world will often do for liberty, without any religious principle. Remember how Greeks, and Romans, and Swiss, and Tyrolese, have endured the loss of all things, and even life itself, rather than bend their necks to a foreign yoke. Let their example provoke you to emulation. If men can do so much for a corruptible crown, how much more should you do for one that is incorruptible! Awake to a sense of the misery of being a slave. For life, and happiness, and liberty, arise and fight.

Fear not to begin and enlist under Christ's banner. The great Captain of your salvation rejects none who come to Him. Like David in the cave of Adullam, He is ready to receive all who apply to Him, however unworthy they may feel themselves. None who repent and believe are too bad to be enrolled in the ranks of Christ's army. All who come to Him by faith are admitted, clothed, armed, trained, and finally led on to complete victory. Fear not to begin this very day. There is yet room for you.

Fear not to go on fighting, if you once enlist. The more thorough and wholehearted you are as a soldier, the more comfortable will you find your warfare. No doubt you will often meet with trouble, fatigue, and hard fighting before your warfare is accomplished. But let none of these things move you. Greater is He who is for you than all they who be against you. Everlasting liberty or everlasting captivity are the alternatives before you. Choose liberty, and fight to the last.

(2) *It may be you know something of the Christian warfare, and are a tried and proved soldier already.* If that be your case, accept a parting word of advice and encouragement from a fellow-soldier. Let me speak to myself as well as to you. Let us stir up our minds by way of remembrance. There are some things that we cannot remember too well.

Let us remember that if we would fight successfully, we must put on the whole armor of God, and never lay it aside till we die. Not a single piece of the armor can be dispensed with. The girdle of truth, the breastplate of righteousness, the shield of faith, the sword of the Spirit, the helmet of hope—each and all are needful. Not a single day can we dispense with any part of this armor. Well says an old veteran in Christ's army, who died two hundred years ago, "In heaven we shall appear, not in armor, but in robes of glory. But here our arms are to be worn night and day. We must walk, work, sleep in them, or else we are not true soldiers of Christ."[2]

Let us remember the solemn words of an inspired warrior, who went to his rest 1,800 years ago: "No man that warreth entangleth himself with the affairs of this life; that he may please him who hath chosen him to be a soldier" (2 Tim. 2:4). May we never forget that saying!

Let us remember that some have seemed good soldiers for a little season, and talked loudly of what they would do, and yet turned back disgracefully in the day of battle.

Let us never forget Balaam, and Judas, and Demas, and Lot's wife. Whatever we are, and however weak, let us be real, genuine, true, and sincere.

Let us remember that the eye of our loving Savior is upon us, morning, noon, and night. He will never suffer us to be tempted above that we are able to bear. He can be touched with the feeling of our infirmities, for He suffered Himself, being tempted. He knows what battles and conflicts are, for He Himself was assaulted by the prince of this world. Having such a High Priest, Jesus the Son of God, let us hold fast our profession (Heb. 4:14).

Let us remember that thousands of soldiers before us have

fought the same battle that we are fighting, and come off more than conquerors through Him who loved them. They overcame by the blood of the Lamb; and so also may we. Christ's arm is quite as strong as ever, and Christ's heart is just as loving as ever. He who saved men and women before us is one who never changes. He is "able to save to the uttermost all who come unto God by him." Then let us cast doubts and fears away. Let us "follow them who through faith and patience inherit the promises," and are waiting for us to join them (Heb. 7:25; 6:12).

Finally, let us remember that the time is short, and the coming of the Lord draws nigh. A few more battles and the last trumpet shall sound, and the Prince of Peace shall come to reign on a renewed earth. A few more struggles and conflicts, and then we shall bid an eternal good-bye to warfare, and to sin, to sorrow, and to death. Then let us fight on to the last, and never surrender. Thus says the Captain of our salvation—"He that overcometh shall inherit all things; and I will be his God, and he shall be my son" (Rev. 21:7).

Let me conclude all with the words of John Bunyan, in one of the most beautiful parts of *Pilgrim's Progress*. He is describing the end of one of his best and holiest pilgrims:

After this it was noised abroad that Mr. Valiant-for-Truth was sent for by a summons, by the same party as the others. And he had this word for a token that the summons was true, "The pitcher was broken at the fountain" (Eccl. 12:6).

When he understood it, he called for his friends, and told them of it. Then said he, "I am going to my Father's house; and though with great difficulty I have got hither, yet now I do not repent me of all the troubles I have been at to arrive where I am. My sword I give to him that shall succeed me in my pilgrimage, and my courage and skill to him that can get it. My marks and scars I carry with me, to be a witness for me that I have fought his battles, who will now be my rewarder." When the day that he must go home was come, many accompanied him to the riverside, into which, as he went down, he said, "O death where is thy sting?" And as he went down deeper, he cried, "O grave, where is thy victory?" So he passed over, and all the trumpets sounded for him on the other side.

May our end be like this! May we never forget that without fighting there can be no holiness while we live, and no crown of glory when we die!

1. Editor's note: Alexander Pope.

2. Gurnall's *Christian Armor*.

5

The Cost

∾

THE TEXT THAT HEADS this page is one of great importance. Few are the people who are not often obliged to ask themselves— "What does it cost?"

In buying property, in building houses, in furnishing rooms, in forming plans, in changing dwellings, in educating children, it is wise and prudent to look forward and consider. Many would save themselves much sorrow and trouble if they would only remember the question—"What does it cost?"

But there is one subject on which it is specially important to "count the cost." That subject is the salvation of our souls. What does it cost to be a true Christian? What does it cost to be a really holy man? This, after all, is the grand question. For want of thought about this, thousands, after seeming to begin well, turn away from the road to heaven, and are lost forever in hell. Let me try to say a few words that may throw light on the subject.

I. I will show, firstly, *what it costs to be a true Christian.*

II. I will explain, secondly, *why it is of such great importance to count the cost.*

III. I will give, in the last place, *some hints that may help men to count the cost rightly.*

We are living in strange times. Events are hurrying on with singular rapidity. We never know "what a day may bring forth"; how much less do we know what may happen in a year! We live in a day of great religious profession. Scores of professing Christians in every part of the land are expressing a desire for more holiness and a higher degree of spiritual life. Yet nothing is more common than to see people receiving the Word with joy, and then after two or three years falling away, and going back to their sins. They had not considered "what it costs" to be a really consistent believer and holy Christian. Surely these are times when we ought often to sit down and "count the cost," and to consider the state of our souls. We must mind what we are about. If we desire to be truly holy, it is a good sign. We may thank God for putting the desire into our hearts. But still the cost ought to be counted. No doubt Christ's way to eternal life is a way of pleasantness. But it is folly to shut our eyes to the fact that His way is narrow, and the cross comes before the crown.

I. I have, first, to show *what it costs to be a true Christian.*

Let there be no mistake about my meaning. I am not examining what it costs to save a Christian's soul. I know well that it costs nothing less than the blood of the Son of God to provide an atonement, and to redeem man from hell. The price paid for our redemption was nothing less than the death of Jesus Christ on Calvary. We "are bought with a price." "Christ gave himself a ransom for all" (1 Cor. 6:20; 1 Tim. 2:6). But all this is wide of the question. The point I want to consider is another one altogether. *It is what a man must be ready to give up* if he wishes to be saved. It is the amount of sacrifice a man must submit to if he intends to serve Christ. It is in this sense that I raise the question, "What does it cost?" And I believe firmly that it is a most important one.

I grant freely that it costs little to be a mere outward Christian. A man has only got to attend a place of worship twice on Sunday, and to be tolerably moral during the week, and he has gone as far as thousands around him ever go in religion. All this is cheap and easy work: it entails no self-denial or self-sacrifice. If this is saving Christianity, and will take us to heaven when we die, we must alter the description of the way of life, and write, "Wide is the gate and broad is the way that leads to heaven!"

But it does cost something to be a real Christian, according to the standard of the Bible. There are enemies to be overcome; battles to be fought, sacrifices to be made, an Egypt to be forsaken, a wilderness to be passed through, a cross to be carried, a race to be run. Conversion is not putting a man in an armchair and taking him easily to heaven. It is the beginning of a mighty conflict, in which it costs much to win the victory. Hence arises the unspeakable importance of "counting the cost."

Let me try to show precisely and particularly what it costs to be a true Christian. Let us suppose that a man is disposed to take service with Christ, and feels drawn and inclined to follow Him. Let us suppose that some affliction, or some sudden death, or an awakening sermon, has stirred his conscience, and made him feel the value of his soul and desire to be a true Christian. No doubt there is everything to encourage him. His sins may be freely forgiven, however many and great. His heart may be completely changed, however cold and hard. Christ and the Holy Spirit, mercy and grace, are all ready for him. But still he should count the cost. Let us see particularly, one by one, the things that his religion will cost him.

(a) For one thing, it will cost him his *self-righteousness.* He must cast away all pride and high thoughts, and conceit of his own goodness. He must be content to go to heaven as a poor sinner saved only by free grace, and owing all to the merit and righteousness of another. He must really feel as well as say the Prayer Book words—that he has "erred and gone astray like a lost sheep," that he has "left undone the things he ought to have done, and done the things he ought not to have done, and that there is no health in him." He must be willing to give up all trust in his own morality, respectability, praying, Bible reading, church going, and sacrament receiving, and to trust in nothing but Jesus Christ.

Now this sounds hard to some. I do not wonder. "Sir," said a godly ploughman to the well-known James Hervey, of Weston Favell, "it is harder to deny proud self than sinful self. But it is absolutely necessary." Let us set down this item first and foremost in our account. To be a true Christian it will cost a man his self-righteousness.

(b) For another thing, it will cost a man his *sins*. He must be willing to give up every habit and practice that is wrong in God's sight. He must set his face against it, quarrel with it, break off from it, fight with it, crucify it, and labor to keep it under, whatever the world around him may say or think. He must do this honestly and fairly. There must be no separate truce with any special sin that he loves. He must count all sins as his deadly enemies, and hate every false way. Whether little or great, whether open or secret, all his sins must be thoroughly renounced. They may struggle hard with him every day, and sometimes almost get the mastery over him. But he must never give way to them. He must keep up a perpetual war with his sins. It is written—"Cast away from you all your transgressions." "Break off thy sins and iniquities." "Cease to do evil" (Ezek. 18:31; Dan. 4:27; Isa. 1:16).

This also sounds hard. I do not wonder. Our sins are often as dear to us as our children: we love them, hug them, cleave to them, and delight in them. To part with them is as hard as cutting off a right hand, or plucking out a right eye. But it must be done. The parting must come. "Though wickedness be sweet in the sinner's mouth, though he hide it under his tongue; though he spare it, and forsake it not," yet it must be given up, if he wishes to be saved (Job 20:12–13). He and sin must quarrel, if he and God are to be friends. Christ is willing to receive any sinners.

But He will not receive them if they will stick to their sins. Let us set down that item second in our account. To be a Christian it will cost a man his sins.

(c) For another thing, it will cost a man his *love of ease.* He must take pains and trouble, if he means to run a successful race toward heaven. He must daily watch and stand on his guard, like a soldier on the enemy's ground. He must take heed to his behavior every hour of the day, in every company, and in every place, in public as well as in private, among strangers as well as at home. He must be careful over his time, his tongue, his temper, his thoughts, his imagination, his motives, his conduct in every relation of life. He must be diligent about his prayers, his Bible reading, and his use of Sundays, with all their means of grace. In attending to these things he may come far short of perfection; but there is none of them that he can safely neglect. "The soul of the sluggard desireth, and hath nothing: but the soul of the diligent shall be made fat" (Prov. 13:4).

This also sounds hard. There is nothing we naturally dislike so much as "trouble" about our religion. We hate trouble. We secretly wish we could have a "vicarious" Christianity, and could be good by proxy, and have everything done for us. Anything that requires exertion and labor is entirely against the grain of our hearts. But the soul can have "no gains without pains." Let us set down that item third in our account. To be a Christian it will cost a man his love of ease.

(d) In the last place, it will cost a man *the favor of the world.*

He must be content to be thought ill of by man if he pleases God. He must count it no strange thing to be mocked, ridiculed, slandered, persecuted, and even hated. He must not be surprised to find his opinions and practices in religion despised and held up to scorn. He must submit to be thought by many a fool, an enthusiast, and a fanatic—to have his words perverted and his actions misrepresented. In fact, he must not marvel if some call him mad. The Master says—"Remember the word that I said unto you, The servant is not greater than his lord. If they have persecuted me, they will also persecute you; if they have kept my saying, they will keep yours also" (John 15:20).

I daresay this also sounds hard. We naturally dislike unjust dealing and false charges, and think it very hard to be accused without cause. We should not be flesh and blood if we did not wish to have the good opinion of our neighbors. It is always unpleasant to be spoken against, and forsaken, and lied about, and to stand alone. But there is no help for it. The cup that our Master drank must be drunk by His disciples. They must be "despised and rejected of men" (Isa. 53:3). Let us set down that item last in our account. To be a Christian it will cost a man the favor of the world.

Such is the account of what it costs to be a true Christian. I grant the list is a heavy one. But where is the item that could be removed? Bold indeed must that man be who would dare to say that we may keep our self-righteousness, our sins, our laziness, and our love of the world, and yet be saved!

I grant it costs much to be a true Christian. But who in his sound senses can doubt that it is worth any cost to have the soul saved? When the ship is in danger of sinking, the crew think nothing of casting overboard the precious cargo. When a limb is dead, a man will submit to any severe operation, and even to amputation, to save life. Surely a Christian should be willing to give up anything that stands between him and heaven. A religion that costs nothing is worth nothing! A cheap Christianity, without a cross, will prove in the end a useless Christianity, without a crown.

II. I have now, in the second place, to explain *why "counting the cost" is of such great importance to man's soul.*

I might easily settle this question by laying down the principle that no duty enjoined by Christ can ever be neglected without damage. I might show how many shut their eyes throughout life to the nature of saving religion, and refuse to consider what it really costs to be a Christian. I might describe how at last, when life is ebbing away, they wake up, and make a few spasmodic efforts to turn to God. I might tell you how they find to their amazement that repentance and conversion are no such easy matters as they had supposed, and that it costs "a great sum" to be a true Christian. They discover that habits of pride and sinful indulgence, and love of ease, and worldliness, are not so easily laid aside as they had dreamed. And so, after a faint struggle, they give up in despair, and leave the world hopeless, graceless, and unfit to meet God! They had flattered themselves all their days that religion would be easy work when they once took it up seriously. But they open their eyes too late, and discover for the first time that they are ruined because they never "counted the cost."

But there is one class of persons to whom especially I wish to address myself in handling this part of my subject. It is a large class—an increasing class—and a class that in these days is in peculiar danger. Let me in a few plain words try to describe this class. It deserves our best attention.

The persons I speak of are not thoughtless about religion; they think a good deal about it. They are not ignorant of religion; they know the outlines of it pretty well. But their great defect is that they are not "rooted and grounded" in their faith. Too often they have picked up their knowledge secondhand, from being in religious families, or from being trained in religious ways, but have never worked it out by their own inward experience. Too often they have hastily taken up a profession of religion under the pressure of circumstances, from sentimental feelings, from animal excitement, or from a vague desire to do like others around them, but without any solid work of grace in their hearts. Persons like these are in a position of immense danger. They are precisely those, if Bible examples are worth anything, who need to be exhorted "to count the cost."

For want of "counting the cost," myriads of the children of Israel perished miserably in the wilderness between Egypt and Canaan. They left Egypt full of zeal and fervor, as if nothing could stop them. But when they found dangers and difficulties in the way, their courage soon cooled down. They had never reckoned on trouble. They had thought the promised land would be all before them in a few days. And so, when enemies, privations, hunger, and thirst began to try them, they murmured against Moses and God, and would fain have gone back to Egypt. In a word, they had "not counted the cost," and so lost everything, and died in their sins.

For want of "counting the cost," many of our Lord Jesus Christ's hearers went back after a time, and "walked no more with him" (John 6:66). When they first saw His miracles and heard His preaching, they thought "the kingdom of God would immediately appear." They cast in their lot with His apostles, and followed Him without thinking of the consequences. But when they found that there were hard doctrines to be believed, and hard work to be done, and hard treatment to be borne, their faith gave way entirely, and proved to be nothing at all. In a word, they had not "counted the cost," and so made shipwreck of their profession.

For want of "counting the cost," King Herod returned to his old sins, and destroyed his soul. He liked to hear John the Baptist preach. He "observed" and honored him as a just and holy man. He even "did many things" that were right and good. But when he found that he must give up his darling Herodias, his religion entirely broke down. He had not reckoned on this (Mark 6:20). He had not "counted the cost."

For want of "counting the cost," Demas forsook the company of St. Paul, forsook the gospel, forsook Christ, forsook heaven.

For a long time he journeyed with the great apostle of the Gentiles, and was actually a "fellow-laborer." But when he found he could not have the friendship of this world as well as the friendship of God, he gave up his Christianity and clave to the world. "Demas hath forsaken me," says St. Paul, "having loved this present world" (2 Tim. 4:10). He had not "counted the cost."

For want of "counting the cost," the hearers of powerful evangelical preachers often come to miserable ends. They are stirred and excited into professing what they have not really experienced. They receive the Word with a "joy" so extravagant that it almost startles old Christians. They run for a time with such zeal and fervor that they seem likely to outstrip all others. They talk and work for spiritual objects with such enthusiasm that they make older believers feel ashamed. But when the novelty and freshness of their feelings is gone, a change comes over them. They prove to have been nothing more than stony-ground hearers. The description the great Master gives in the Parable of the Sower is exactly exemplified. "Temptation or persecution arises because of the Word, and they are offended" (Matt. 13:21). Little by little their zeal melts away, and their love becomes cold. By and by their seats are empty in the assembly of God's people, and they are heard of no more among Christians. And why? They had never "counted the cost."

For want of "counting the cost," hundreds of professed converts, under religious revivals, go back to the world after a time, and bring disgrace on religion. They begin with a sadly mistaken notion of what is true Christianity. They fancy it consists in nothing more than a so-called "coming to Christ," and having strong inward feelings of joy and peace. And so, when they find, after a time, that there is a cross to be carried, that our hearts are deceitful, and that there is a busy devil always near us, they cool down in disgust, and return to their old sins. And why? Because they had really never known what Bible Christianity is. They had never learned that we must "count the cost."[1]

For want of "counting the cost," the children of religious parents often turn out ill, and bring disgrace on Christianity. Familiar from their earliest years with the form and theory of the gospel—taught even from infancy to repeat great leading text, accustomed every week to be instructed in the gospel, or to instruct others in Sunday schools—they often grow up professing a religion without knowing why, or without ever having thought seriously about it. And then when the realities of grown-up life begin to press upon them, they often astound everyone by dropping all their religion and plunging right into the world. And why? They had never thoroughly understood the sacrifices that Christianity entails. They had never been taught to "count the cost."

These are solemn and painful truths. But they are truths. They all help to show the immense importance of the subject I am now considering. They all point out the absolute necessity of pressing the subject of this chapter on all who profess a desire for holiness, and of crying aloud in all the churches—"Count the cost."

I am bold to say that it would be well if the duty of "count-ing the cost" were more frequently taught than it is. Impatient hurry is the order of the day with many religionists. Instantaneous conversions, and immediate sensible peace, are the only results they seem to care for from the gospel. Compared with these, all other things are thrown into the shade. To produce them is the grand end and object, apparently, of all their labors. I say without hesitation that such a naked, one-sided mode of teaching Christianity is mischievous in the extreme.

Let no one mistake my meaning. I thoroughly approve of offering men a full, free, present, immediate salvation in Christ Jesus. I thoroughly approve of urging on man the possibility and the duty of immediate, instantaneous conversion. In these mat-ters I give place to no one. But I do say that these truths ought not to be set before men nakedly, singly, and alone. They ought to be told honestly what it is they are taking up, if they profess a desire to come out from the world and serve Christ. They ought not to be pressed into the ranks of Christ's army without being told what the warfare entails. In a word, they should be told honestly to "count the cost."

Does anyone ask what our Lord Jesus Christ's practice was in this matter? Let him read what St. Luke records. He tells us that on a certain occasion, "There went great multitudes with him: and he turned and said unto them, If any come to me, and hate not his father, and mother, and wife, and children, and brethren, and sisters, yea, and his own life also, he cannot be my disciple.

And whosoever doth not bear his cross and come after me, cannot be my disciple" (Luke 14:25–27). I must plainly say, that I cannot reconcile this passage with the proceedings of many modern religious teachers. And yet, to my mind, the doctrine of it is as clear as the sun at noonday. It shows us that we ought not to hurry men into professing discipleship, without warning them plainly to "count the cost."

Does anyone ask what the practice of the eminent and best preachers of the gospel has been in days gone by? I am bold to say that they have all with one mouth borne testimony to the wisdom of our Lord's dealing with the multitudes to which I have just referred. Luther, and Latimer, and Baxter, and Wesley, and Whitefield, and Berridge, and Rowland Hill were all keenly alive to the deceitfulness of man's heart. They knew full well that all is not gold that glitters, that conviction is not conversion, that feeling is not faith, that sentiment is not grace, that all blossoms do not come to fruit. "Be not deceived," was their constant cry. "Consider well what you do. Do not run before you are called. Count the cost."

If we desire to do good, let us never be ashamed of walking in the steps of our Lord Jesus Christ. Work hard if you will, and have the opportunity, for the souls of others. Press them to consider their ways. Compel them with holy violence to come in, to lay down their arms, and to yield themselves to God. Offer them salvation, ready, free, full, immediate salvation. Press Christ and all His benefits on their acceptance. But in all your work tell the truth, and the whole truth. Be ashamed to use the vulgar arts of a recruiting sergeant. Do not speak only of the uniform, the pay, and the glory; speak also of the enemies, the battle, the armor, the watching, the marching, and the drill. Do not present only one side of Christianity. Do not keep back "the cross" of self-denial that must be carried, when you speak of the cross on which Christ died for our redemption. Explain fully what Christianity entails. Entreat men to repent and come to Christ; but bid them at the same time to "count the cost."

III. The third and last thing that I propose to do is *to give some hints that may help men to "count the cost" rightly.*

Sorry indeed should I be if I did not say something on this branch of my subject. I have no wish to discourage anyone, or to keep anyone back from Christ's service. It is my heart's desire to encourage everyone to go forward and take up the cross. Let us "count the cost" by all means, and count it carefully. But let us remember, that if we count rightly, and look on all sides, there is nothing that need make us afraid.

Let us mention some things that should always enter into our calculations in counting the cost of true Christianity. Set down honestly and fairly what you will have to give up and go through, if you become Christ's disciple. Leave nothing out. Put it all down. But then set down side by side the following sums, which I am going to give you. Do this fairly and correctly, and I am not afraid for the result.

(a) Count up and compare, for one thing, *the profit and the* *loss,* if you are a truehearted and holy Christian. You may possibly lose something in this world, but you will gain the salvation of your immortal soul. It is written—"What shall it profit a man, if he shall gain the whole world, and lose his own soul?" (Mark 8:36).

(b) Count up and compare, for another thing, *the praise and the blame,* if you are a truehearted and holy Christian. You may possibly be blamed by man, but you will have the praise of God the Father, God the Son, and God the Holy Ghost. Your blame will come from the lips of a few erring, blind, fallible men and women. Your praise will come from the King of kings and Judge of all the earth. It is only those whom He blesses who are really blessed. It is written—"Blessed are ye when men shall revile you, and persecute you, and say all manner of evil against you falsely, for my sake. Rejoice and be exceeding glad, for great is your reward in heaven" (Matt. 5:11–12).

(c) Count up and compare, for another thing, the friends and the enemies, if you are a truehearted and holy Christian. On the one side of you is the enmity of the devil and the wicked. On the other, you have the favor and friendship of the Lord Jesus Christ. Your enemies, at most, can only bruise your heel. They may rage loudly, and compass sea and land to work your ruin; but they cannot destroy you. Your Friend is able to save to the uttermost all them who come unto God by Him. None shall ever pluck His sheep out of His hand. It is written—"Be not afraid of them that kill the body, and after that have no more that they can do. But I will forewarn you whom ye shall fear: fear him, which after he hath killed hath power to cast into hell; yea, I say unto you, fear him" (Luke 12:4–5).

(d) Count up and compare, for another thing, *the life that now is and the life to come*, if you are a truehearted and holy Christian. The time present, no doubt, is not a time of ease. It is a time of watching and praying, fighting and struggling, believing and working. But it is only for a few years. The time future is the season of rest and refreshing. Sin shall be cast out. Satan shall be bound. And, best of all, it shall be a rest forever. It is written— "Our light affliction, which is but for a moment, worketh for us a far more exceeding and eternal weight of glory; while we look not at the things which are seen, but at the things which are not seen: for the things which are seen are temporal; but the things which are not seen are eternal" (2 Cor. 4:17–18).

(e) Count up and compare, for another thing, *the pleasures of sin and the happiness of God's service*, if you are a truehearted and holy Christian. The pleasures that the worldly man gets by his ways are hollow, unreal, and unsatisfying. They are like the fire of thorns, flashing and crackling for a few minutes, and then quenched forever. The happiness that Christ gives to His people is something solid, lasting, and substantial. It is not dependent on health or circumstances. It never leaves a man, even in death. It ends in a crown of glory that fades not away. It is written—"The joy of the hypocrite is but for a moment." "As the crackling of thorns under a pot, so is the laughter of the fool" (Job 20:5; Eccl.

7:6). But it is also written—"Peace I leave with you, my peace give I unto you: not as the world giveth, give I unto you. Let not your heart be troubled, neither let it be afraid" (John 14:27).

(f) Count up and compare, for another thing, *the trouble that true Christianity entails, and the troubles that are in store for the wicked beyond the grave.* Grant for a moment that Bible reading, and praying, and repenting, and believing, and holy living require pains and self-denial. It is all nothing compared to that "wrath to come," which is stored up for the impenitent and unbelieving. A single day in hell will be worse than a whole life spent in carrying the cross. The "worm that never dies, and the fire that is not quenched" are things that it passes man's power to conceive fully or describe. It is written—"Son, remember that thou in thy lifetime receivedst thy good things, and likewise Lazarus evil things; but now he is comforted and thou art tormented" (Luke 16:25).

(g) Count up and compare, in the last place, *the number of those who turn from sin and the world and serve Christ, and the number of those who forsake Christ and return to the world.* On the one side you will find thousands—on the other you will find none. Multitudes are every year turning out of the broad way and entering the narrow. None who really enter the narrow way grow tired of it and return to the broad. The footsteps in the downward road are often to be seen turning out of it. The footsteps in the road to heaven are all one way. It is written—"The way of the wicked is darkness." "The way of transgressors is hard" (Prov.

4:19; 13:15). But it is also written—"The path of the just is as the shining light, which shineth more and more unto the perfect day" (Prov. 4:18).

Such sums as these, no doubt, are often not done correctly. Not a few, I am well aware, are ever "halting between two opinions." They cannot make up their minds that it is worthwhile to serve Christ. The losses and gains, the advantages and disadvantages, the sorrows and the joys, the helps and the hindrances, appear to them so nearly balanced that they cannot decide for God. They cannot do this great sum correctly. They cannot make the result so clear as it ought to be. They do not count right.

But what is the secret of their mistakes? It is want of faith. To come to a right conclusion about our souls, we must have some of that mighty principle that St. Paul describes in the eleventh chapter of his epistle to the Hebrews. Let me try to show how that principle operates in the great business of "counting the cost."

How was it that Noah persevered in building the ark? He stood alone amidst a world of sinners and unbelievers. He had to endure scorn, ridicule, and mockery. What was it that nerved his arm, and made him patiently work on and face it all? It was faith. He believed in a wrath to come. He believed that there was no safety, excepting in the ark that he was preparing. Believing, he held the world's opinion very cheap. He "counted the cost" by faith, and had no doubt that to build the ark was gain.

How was it that Moses forsook the pleasures of Pharaoh's

house, and refused to be called the son of Pharaoh's daughter? How was it that he cast in his lot with a despised people like the Hebrews, and risked everything in this world in carrying out the great work of their deliverance from bondage? To the eye of sense he was losing everything and gaining nothing. What was it that moved him? It was faith. He believed that there was One far above Pharaoh, who would carry him safe through all his undertaking. He believed that the "recompense of reward" was far better than all the honors of Egypt. He "counted the cost" by faith, as "seeing him that is invisible," and was persuaded that to forsake Egypt and go forth into the wilderness was gain.

How was it that Saul the Pharisee could ever make up his mind to become a Christian? The cost and sacrifices of the change were fearfully great. He gave up all his brilliant prospects among his own people. He brought on himself, instead of man's favor, man's hatred, man's enmity, and man's persecution, even unto death. What was it that enabled him to face it all? It was faith. He believed that Jesus, who met him on the way to Damascus, could give him a hundredfold more than he gave up, and in the world to come everlasting life. By faith he "counted the cost," and saw clearly on which side the balance lay. He believed firmly that to carry the cross of Christ was gain.

Let us mark well these things. That faith that made Noah, Moses, and St. Paul do what they did, that faith is the great secret of coming to a right conclusion about our souls. That same faith must be our helper and ready-reckoner, when we sit down to count the cost of being a true Christian. That same faith is to be had for the asking. "He giveth more grace" (James 4:6). Armed with that faith, we shall set things down at their true value. Filled with that faith, we shall neither add to the cross nor subtract from the crown. Our conclusions will be all correct. Our sum total will be without error.

(1) In conclusion, let every reader of this chapter think seriously, *whether his religion costs him anything at present.* Very likely it costs you nothing. Very probably it neither costs you trouble, nor time, nor thought, nor care, nor pains, nor reading, nor praying, nor self-denial, nor conflict, nor working, nor labor of any kind. Now mark what I say. Such a religion as this will never save your soul. It will never give you peace while you live, nor hope while you die. It will not support you in the day of affliction, nor cheer you in the hour of death. A religion that costs nothing is worth nothing. Awake before it is too late. Awake and repent. Awake and be converted. Awake and believe. Awake and pray. Rest not till you can give a satisfactory answer to my question, "What does it cost?"

(2) Think, if you want stirring motives for serving God, *what it cost to provide a salvation for your soul.* Think how the Son of God left heaven and became Man, suffered on the cross, and lay in the grave, to pay your debt to God, and work out for you a complete redemption. Think of all this and learn that it is no light matter to possess an immortal soul. It is worthwhile to take some trouble about one's soul.

Ah, lazy man or woman, is it really come to this, that you

will miss heaven for lack of trouble? Are you really determined to make shipwreck forever, from mere dislike to exertion? Away with the cowardly, unworthy thought. Arise and play the man. Say to yourself, "Whatever it may cost, I will, at any rate, strive to enter in at the strait gate." Look at the cross of Christ, and take fresh courage. Look forward to death, judgment, and eternity, and be in earnest. It may cost much to be a Christian, but you may be sure it pays.

(3) If any reader of this book really feels that he has counted the cost, and taken up the cross, I bid him *persevere and press on.* I daresay you often feel your heart faint, and are sorely tempted to give up in despair. Your enemies seem so many, your besetting sins so strong, your friends so few, the way so steep and narrow, you hardly know what to do. But still I say, persevere and press on.

The time is very short. A few more years of watching and praying, a few more tossings on the sea of this world, a few more deaths and changes, a few more winters and summers, and all will be over. We shall have fought our last battle, and shall need to fight no more.

The presence and company of Christ will make amends for all we suffer here below. When we see as we have been seen, and look back on the journey of life, we shall wonder at our own faintness of heart. We shall marvel that we made so much of our cross, and thought so little of our crown. We shall marvel that in "counting the cost" we could ever doubt on which side the balance of profit lay. Let us take courage. We are not far from home. *It may cost much to be a true Christian and a consistent believer; but it pays.*[1]

1. I should be very sorry indeed if the language I have used on pages 149–51 about *revivals* was misunderstood. To prevent this I will offer a few remarks by way of explanation.

For true revivals of religion no one can be more deeply thankful than I am. Wherever they may take place, and by whatever agents they may be effected, I desire to bless God for them, with all my heart. "If Christ is preached," I rejoice, whoever may be the preacher. If souls are saved, I rejoice, by whatever section of the Church the word of life has been ministered.

But it is a melancholy fact that, in a world like this, you cannot have good without evil. I have no hesitation in saying, that one consequence of the revival movement has been the rise of a theological system that I feel obliged to call defective and mischievous in the extreme.

The leading feature of the theological system I refer to is this: an extravagant and disproportionate magnifying of three points in religion—viz., instantaneous conversion—the invitation of unconverted sinners to come to Christ—and the possession of inward joy and peace as a test of conversion. I repeat that these three grand truths (for truths they are) are so incessantly and exclusively brought forward, in some quarters, that great harm is done.

Instantaneous conversion, no doubt, ought to be pressed on people. But surely they ought not to be led to suppose that there is no other sort of conversion, and that unless they are suddenly and powerfully converted to God, they are not converted at all.

The duty of coming to Christ at once, "just as we are," should be pressed on all hearers. It is the very cornerstone of Gospel preaching. But surely men ought to be told to repent as well as to believe. They should be told why they are to come to Christ, and what they are to come for, and whence their need arises.

The nearness of peace and comfort in Christ should be proclaimed to men. But surely they should be taught that the possession of strong inward joys and high frames of mind is not essential to justification, and that there may be true faith and true peace without such very triumphant feelings. Joy alone is no certain evidence of grace.

The defects of the theological system I have in view appear to me to be these: (1) The work of the Holy Ghost in converting sinners is far too much narrowed and confined to one single way. Not all true converts are converted instantaneously, like Saul and the Philippian jailor. (2) Sinners are not sufficiently instructed about the holiness of God's law, the depth of their sinfulness, and the real guilt of sin. To be incessantly telling a sinner to "come to Christ" is of little use, unless you tell him why he needs to come, and show him fully his sins. (3) Faith is not properly explained. In some cases people are taught that mere feeling is faith! At this rate the very devils are believers! (4) The possession of inward joy and assurance is made essential to believing. Yet assurance is certainly not of the essence of saving faith. There may be faith when there is no assurance. To insist on all believers at once "rejoicing," as soon as they believe, is most unsafe. Some, I am quite sure, will rejoice without believing, while others will believe who cannot at once rejoice. (5) Last, but not least, the sovereignty of God in saving sinners, and the absolute necessity of prevenient grace, are far too much overlooked. Many talk as if conversions could be manufactured at man's pleasure, and as if there were no such text as this, "It is not of him that willeth, nor of him that runneth, but of God that showeth mercy" (Rom. 9:16).

The mischief done by the theological system I refer to is, I am persuaded, very great. On the one hand, many humble-minded Christians are totally discouraged and daunted. They fancy they have no grace because they cannot reach up to the high frames and feelings that are pressed on their attention. On the other side, many graceless people are deluded into thinking they are "converted," because under the pressure of animal excitement and temporary feelings they are led to profess themselves Christians. And all this time the thoughtless and ungodly look on with contempt, and find fresh reasons for neglecting religion altogether.

The antidotes to the state of things I deplore are plain and few. (1) Let "all the counsel of God be taught" in Scriptural proportion; and let not two or three precious doctrines of the Gospel be allowed to overshadow all other truths. (2) Let repentance be taught fully as well as faith, and not thrust completely into the background. Our Lord Jesus Christ and St. Paul always taught both. (3) Let the variety of the Holy Ghost's works be honestly stated and admitted; and while instantaneous conversion is pressed on men, let it not be taught as a necessity. (4) Let those who profess to have found immediate sensible peace be plainly warned to try themselves well, and to remember that feeling is not faith, and the "patient continuance in well-doing" is the great proof that faith is true (John 8:31). (5) Let the great duty of "counting the cost" be constantly urged on all who are disposed to make a religious profession, and let them be honestly and fairly told that there is warfare as well as peace, a cross as well as a crown, in Christ's service.

I am sure that unhealthy excitement is above all things to be dreaded in reli-

JhC. RYLE ~ 161

gion, because it often ends in fatal, soul-ruining reaction and utter deadness. And when multitudes are suddenly brought under the power of religious impressions, unhealthy excitement is almost sure to follow.

I have not much faith in the soundness of conversions when they are said to take places in masses and wholesale. It does not seem to me in harmony with God's general dealings in this dispensation. To my eyes it appears that God's ordinary place is to call in individuals one by one. Therefore, when I hear of large numbers being suddenly converted all at one time, I hear of it with less hope than some. The healthiest and most enduring success in mission fields is certainly not where natives have come over to Christianity in a mass. The most satisfactory and firmest work at home does not always appear to me to be the work done in revivals.

There are two passages of Scripture that I should like to have frequently and fully expounded in the present day by all who preach the Gospel, and especially by those who have anything to do with revivals. One passage is the parable of the sower. That parable is not recorded three times over without good reason and a deep meaning.—The other passage is our Lord's teaching about "counting the cost," and the words that He spoke to the "great multitudes" whom He saw following Him. It is very noteworthy that He did not on that occasion say anything to flatter these volunteers or encourage them to follow Him. No: He saw what their case needed. He told them to stand still and "count the cost" (Luke 14:25, etc.). I am not sure that some modern preachers would have adopted this course of treatment.

6

Growth

∾

"GROW IN GRACE, AND IN THE KNOWLEDGE OF
OUR LORD AND SAVIOR JESUS CHRIST." *(2 Peter 3:18)*

THE SUBJECT OF THE TEXT that heads this page is one that I dare not omit in this volume about holiness. It is one that ought to be deeply interesting to every true Christian. It naturally raises the questions: Do we grow in grace? Do we get on in our religion? Do we make progress?

To a mere formal Christian I cannot expect the inquiry to seem worth attention. The man who has nothing more than a kind of Sunday religion—whose Christianity is like his Sunday clothes, put on once a week, and then laid aside—such a man cannot, of course, be expected to care about "growth in grace." He knows nothing about such matters. "They are foolishness to him" (1 Cor. 2:14). But to everyone who is in downright earnest about his soul, and hungers and thirsts after spiritual life, the question ought to come home with searching power. Do we make progress in our religion? Do we grow?

The question is one that is always useful, but especially so at certain seasons. A Saturday night, a Communion Sunday, the return of a birthday, the end of a year—all these are seasons that ought to set us thinking, and make us look within. Time is fast flying. Life is fast ebbing away. The hour is daily drawing nearer when the reality of our Christianity will be tested, and it will be seen whether we have built on "the rock" or on "the sand." Surely it becomes us from time to time to examine ourselves, and take account of our souls? Do we get on in spiritual things? Do we grow?

The question is one that is of special importance in the present day. Crude and strange opinions are floating in men's minds on some points of doctrine, and among others on the point of "growth in grace," as an essential part of true holiness. By some it is totally denied. By others it is explained away, and pared down to nothing. By thousands it is misunderstood, and consequently neglected. In a day like this it is useful to look fairly in the face the whole subject of Christian growth.

In considering this subject there are three things that I wish to bring forward and establish:

    I. *The reality of religious growth.* There is such a thing as "growth in grace."

    II. *The marks of religious growth.* There are marks by which growth in grace may be known.

    III. *The means of religious growth.* There are means that must be used by those who desire growth in grace.

I know not who you are, into whose hands this book may have fallen. But I am not ashamed to ask your best attention to its contents. Believe me, the subject is no mere matter of speculation and controversy. It is an eminently practical subject, if any is in religion. It is intimately and inseparably connected with the whole question of "sanctification." It is a leading mark of true saints that they grow. The spiritual health and prosperity, the spiritual happiness and comfort of every truehearted and holy Christian, are intimately connected with the subject of spiritual growth.

I. The first point I propose to establish is this: *There is such a thing as growth in grace.*

That any Christian should deny this proposition is at first sight a strange and melancholy thing. But it is fair to remember that man's understanding is fallen no less than his will. Disagreements about doctrines are often nothing more than disagreements about the meaning of words. I try to hope that it is so in the present case. I try to believe that when I speak of growth in grace and maintain it, I mean one thing, while my brethren who deny it mean quite another. Let me therefore clear the way by explaining what I mean.

When I speak of growth in grace, I do not for a moment mean that a believer's interest in Christ can grow. I do not mean that he can grow in safety, acceptance with God, or security. I do not mean that he can ever be more justified, more pardoned, more forgiven, more at peace with God, than he is the first moment that he believes. I hold firmly that the justification of a believer is a finished, perfect, and complete work; and that the weakest saint, though he may not know and feel it, is as completely justified as the strongest. I hold firmly that our election, calling, and standing in Christ admit of no degrees, increase, or diminution. If anyone dreams that by growth in grace I mean growth in justification, he is utterly wide of the mark, and utterly mistaken about the whole point I am considering. I would go to the stake, God helping me, for the glorious truth, that in the matter of justification before God every believer is "complete in Christ" (Col. 2:10). Nothing can be added to his justification from the moment he believes, and nothing taken away.

When I speak of growth in grace, I only mean increase in the degree, size, strength, vigor, and power of the graces, which the Holy Spirit plants in a believer's heart. I hold that every one of those graces admits of growth, progress, and increase. I hold that repentance, faith, hope, love, humility, zeal, courage, and the like, may be little or great, strong or weak, vigorous or feeble, and may vary greatly in the same man at different periods of his life. When I speak of a man growing in grace, I mean simply this—that his sense of sin is becoming deeper, his faith stronger, his hope brighter, his love more extensive, his spiritual-mindedness more marked. He feels more of the power of godliness in his own heart. He manifests more of it in his life. He is going on from strength to strength, from faith to faith, and from grace to grace. I leave it to others to describe such a man's condition by any words they please. For myself I think the truest and best account of him is this—he is growing in grace.

One principal ground on which I build this doctrine of growth in grace is the plain language of Scripture. If words in the Bible mean anything, there is such a thing as growth, and believers ought to be exhorted to grow. What says St. Paul? "Your faith groweth exceedingly" (2 Thess. 1:3). "We beseech you brethren, that ye increase more and more" (1 Thess. 4:10). "Increasing in the knowledge of God" (Col. 1:10). "Having hope, when your faith is increased" (2 Cor. 10:15). "The Lord make you to increase in love" (1 Thess. 3:12). "That ye may grow up into him in all things" (Eph. 4:15). "I pray that your love may abound more and more" (Phil. 1:9). "We beseech you, as ye have received of us how ye ought to walk and to please God, so ye would abound more and more" (1 Thess. 4:1). What says St. Peter? "Desire the sincere milk of the Word, that ye may grow thereby" (1 Pet. 2:2). "Grow in grace, and in the knowledge of our Lord and Savior Jesus Christ" (2 Pet. 3:18). I know not what others think of such texts. To me they seem to establish the doctrine for which I contend, and to be incapable of any other explanation. Growth in grace is taught in the Bible. I might stop here and say no more.

The other ground, however, on which I build the doctrine of growth in grace, is the ground of fact and experience. I ask any honest reader of the New Testament whether he cannot see degrees of grace in the New Testament saints whose histories are recorded, as plainly as the sun at noonday? I ask him whether he cannot see in the very same persons as great a difference between their faith and knowledge at one time and at another, as between the same man's strength when he is an infant and when he is a grown-up man? I ask him whether the Scripture does not distinctly recognize this in the language it uses, when it speaks of "weak" faith and "strong" faith, and of Christians as "newborn babes," "little children," "young men," and "fathers"? (1 Pet. 2:2; 1 John 2:12–14). I ask him, above all, whether his own observation of believers, nowadays, does not bring him to the same conclusion? What true Christian would not confess that there is as much difference between the degree of his own faith and knowledge when he was first converted, and his present attainments, as there is between a sapling and a full-grown tree? His graces are the same in principle; but they have grown. I know not how these facts strike others: to my eyes they seem to prove, most unanswerably, that growth in grace is a real thing.

I feel almost ashamed to dwell so long upon this part of my subject. In fact, if any man means to say that the faith, and hope, and knowledge, and holiness of a newly converted person are as strong as those of an old-established believer, and need no increase, it is waste of time to argue further. No doubt they are as real, but not so strong—as true, but not so vigorous—as much seeds of the Spirit's planting, but not yet so fruitful. And if anyone asks how they are to become stronger, I say it must be by the same process by which all things having life increase—they must grow. And this is what I mean by growth in grace.[1]

Let us turn away from the things I have been discussing to a more practical view of the great subject before us. I want men to look at growth in grace as a thing of infinite importance to the soul. I believe, whatever others may think, that our best interests are concerned in a right view of the question—Do we grow?

(a) Let us know then that growth in grace is the best evidence of spiritual *health* and prosperity. In a child, or a flower, or a tree, we are all aware that when there is no growth there is something wrong. Healthy life in an animal or a vegetable will always show itself by progress and increase.

It is just the same with our souls. If they are progressing and doing well, they will grow.[2]

(b) Let us know, furthermore, that growth in grace is one way to be *happy* in our religion. God has wisely linked together our comfort and our increase in holiness. He has graciously made it our interest to press on and aim high in our Christianity. There is a vast difference between the amount of sensible enjoyment that one believer has in his religion compared to another. But you may be sure that ordinarily the man who feels the most "joy and peace in believing," and has the clearest witness of the Spirit in his heart, is the man who grows.

(c) Let us know, furthermore, that growth in grace is one secret of *usefulness* to others. Our influence on others for good depends greatly on what they see in us. The children of the world measure Christianity quite as much by their eyes as by their ears. The Christian who is always at a standstill, to all appearances the same man, with the same little faults, and weaknesses, and be-setting sins, and petty infirmities, is seldom the Christian who does much good. The man who shakes and stirs minds, and sets the world thinking, is the believer who is continually improving and going forward. Men think there is life and reality when they see growth.[3]

(d) Let us know, furthermore, that growth in grace *pleases* God. It may seem a wonderful thing, no doubt, that anything done by such creatures as we are can give pleasure to the most high God. But so it is. The Scripture speaks of walking so as to "please God." The Scripture says there are sacrifices with which "God is well pleased" (1 Thess. 4:1; Heb. 13:16). The husband-man loves to see the plants on which he has bestowed labor flour-ishing and bearing fruit. It cannot but disappoint and grieve him to see them stunted and standing still. Now what does our Lord Himself say? "I am the true vine, and my Father is the husband-man." "Herein is my Father glorified, that ye bear much fruit; so shall ye be my disciples" (John 15:1, 8). The Lord takes pleasure in all His people—but specially in those who grow.

(e) Let us know, above all, that growth in grace is not only a thing *possible*, but a thing for which believers are *accountable*. To tell an unconverted man, dead in sins, to grow in grace would doubtless be absurd. To tell a believer, who is quickened and alive to God, to grow, is only summoning him to a plain scriptural duty. He has a new principle within him, and it is a solemn duty not to quench it. Neglect of growth robs him of privileges, grieves the Spirit, and makes the chariot wheels of his soul move heavily. Whose fault is it, I should like to know, if a believer does not grow in grace? The fault, I am sure, cannot be laid on God. He delights to "give more grace"; He "hath pleasure in the prosperity of his servants" (James 4:6; Ps. 35:27). The fault, no doubt, is our own. We ourselves are to blame, and none else, if we do not grow.

II. The second point I propose to establish is this: *There are marks by which growth in grace may be known.*

Let me take it for granted that we do not question the reality of growth in grace and its vast importance. So far so good. But you now want to know how anyone may find out whether he is growing in grace or not? I answer that question, in the first place, by observing that we are very poor judges of our own condition, and that bystanders often know us better than we know ourselves. But I answer further, that there are undoubtedly certain great marks and signs of growth in grace, and that wherever you see these marks you see a growing soul. I will now proceed to place some of these marks before you in order.

(a) One mark of growth in grace is increased humility. The man whose soul is growing feels his own sinfulness and unworthiness more every year. He is ready to say with Job, "I am vile" —and with Abraham, I am "dust and ashes"—and with Jacob, "I am not worthy of the least of all thy mercies"—and with David, "I am a worm"—and with Isaiah, "I am a man of unclean lips"— and with Peter, "I am a sinful man, O Lord" (Job 40:4; Gen. 18:27;

32:10; Ps. 22:6; Isa. 6:5; Luke 5:8). The nearer he draws to God, and the more he sees of God's holiness and perfection, the more thoroughly is he sensible of his own countless imperfections. The further he journeys in the way to heaven, the more he understands what St. Paul means when he says, "I am not already perfect"—"I am not meet to be called an apostle"—"I am less than the least of all saints"—"I am chief of sinners" (Phil. 3:12; 1 Cor. 15:9; Eph. 3:8; 1 Tim. 1:15). The riper he is for glory, the more, like the ripe grain, he hangs down his head. The brighter and clearer is his light, the more he sees of the shortcomings and infirmities of his own heart. When first converted, he would tell you he saw but little of them compared to what he sees now. Would anyone know whether he is growing in grace? Be sure that you look within for increased humility.[4]

(b) Another mark of growth in grace is increased *faith and love toward our Lord Jesus Christ.* The man whose soul is growing finds more in Christ to rest upon every year, and rejoices more that he has such a Savior. No doubt he saw much in Him when first he believed. His faith laid hold on the atonement of Christ and gave him hope. But as he grows in grace, he sees a thousand things in Christ of which at first he never dreamed. His love and power—His heart and His intentions—His offices as Substitute, Intercessor, Priest, Advocate, Physician, Shepherd, and Friend, unfold themselves to a growing soul in an unspeakable manner. In short, he discovers a suitableness in Christ to the wants of his soul, of which the half was once not known to him.

Would anyone know if he is growing in grace? Then let him look within for increased knowledge of Christ.

(c) Another mark of growth in grace is increased *holiness of life and conversation.* The man whose soul is growing gets more dominion over sin, the world, and the devil every year. He becomes more careful about his temper, his words, and his actions. He is more watchful over his conduct in every relation of life. He strives more to be conformed to the image of Christ in all things, and to follow Him as his example, as well as to trust in Him as his Savior. He is not content with old attainments and former grace. He forgets the things that are behind and reaches forth unto those things that are before, making "Higher! Upward! Forward! Onward!" his continual motto (Phil. 3:13). On earth he thirsts and longs to have a will more entirely in unison with God's will. In heaven the chief thing that he looks for, next to the presence of Christ, is complete separation from all sin. Would anyone know if he is growing in grace? Then let him look within for increased holiness.[5]

(d) Another mark of growth in grace is increased *spirituality of taste and mind.* The man whose soul is growing takes more interest in spiritual things every year. He does not neglect his duty in the world. He discharges faithfully, diligently, and conscientiously every relation of life, whether at home or abroad. But the things he loves best are spiritual things. The ways, and fashions, and amusements, and recreations of the world have a continually decreasing place in his heart. He does not condemn them as downright sinful, nor say that those who have anything to do with them are going to hell. He only feels that they have a constantly diminishing hold on his own affections, and gradually seem smaller and more trifling in his eyes. Spiritual companions, spiritual occupations, spiritual conversation, appear of ever-increasing value to him. Would anyone know if he is growing in grace? Then let him look within for increasing spirituality of taste.[6]

(e) Another mark of growth in grace is increase of *charity*. The man whose soul is growing is more full of love every year— of love to all men, but especially of love toward the brethren. His love will show itself actively in a growing disposition to do kindnesses, to take trouble for others, to be good-natured to everybody, to be generous, sympathizing, thoughtful, tenderhearted, and considerate. It will show itself passively in a growing disposition to be meek and patient toward all men, to put up with provocation and not stand upon rights, to bear and forbear much rather than quarrel. A growing soul will try to put the best construction on other people's conduct, and to believe all things and hope all things, even to the end. There is no surer mark of backsliding and falling off in grace than an increasing disposition to find fault, pick holes, and see weak points in others. Would anyone know if he is growing in grace? Then let him look within for increasing charity.

(f) One more mark of growth in grace is increased *zeal and diligence in trying to do good to souls.* The man who is really growing will take greater interest in the salvation of sinners every year. Missions at home and abroad, efforts to increase religious light and diminish religious darkness—all these things will every year have a greater place in his attention. He will not become "weary in well-doing" because he does not see every effort succeed. He will not care less for the progress of Christ's cause on earth as he grows older, though he will learn to expect less. He will just work on, whatever the result may be—giving, praying, preaching, speaking, visiting, according to his position— and count his work its own reward. One of the surest marks of spiritual decline is a decreased interest about the souls of others and the growth of Christ's kingdom. Would anyone know whether he is growing in grace? Then let him look within for increased concern about the salvation of souls.

Such are the most trustworthy marks of growth in grace. Let us examine them carefully, and consider what we know about them. I can well believe that they will not please some professing Christians in the present day. Those high-flying religionists, whose only notion of Christianity is that of a state of perpetual joy and ecstasy—who tell you that they have got far beyond the region of conflict and soul humiliation—such persons no doubt will regard the marks I have laid down as "legal," "carnal," and "gendering to bondage." I cannot help that. I call no man master in these things. I only wish my statements to be tried in the balance of Scripture. And I firmly believe that what I have said is not only scriptural, but agreeable to the experience of the most eminent saints in every age. Show me a man in whom the six marks I have mentioned can be found. He is the man who can give a satisfactory answer to the question, *do we grow?*

III. The third and last thing I propose to consider is this: *The means that must be used by those who desire to grow in grace.* The words of St. James must never be forgotten: "Every good gift and every perfect gift is from above, and cometh down from the Father of lights" (James 1:17). This is no doubt as true of growth in grace as it is of everything else. It is the "gift of God." But still it must always be kept in mind that God is pleased to work by means. God has ordained means as well as ends. He who would grow in grace must use the means of growth.[7]

This is a point, I fear, that is too much overlooked by believers. Many admire growth in grace in others, and wish that they themselves were like them. But they seem to suppose that those who grow are what they are by some special gift or grant from God, and that as this gift is not bestowed on themselves they must be content to sit still. This is a grievous delusion, and one against which I desire to testify with all my might. I wish it to be distinctly understood that growth in grace is bound up with the use of means within the reach of all believers, and that, as a general rule, growing souls are what they are because they use these means.

Let me ask the special attention of my readers while I try to set forth in order the means of growth. Cast away forever the vain thought that if a believer does not grow in grace it is not his fault.

Settle it in your mind that a believer, a man quickened by the Spirit, is not a mere dead creature, but a being of mighty capacities and responsibilities. Let the words of Solomon sink down into your heart: "The soul of the diligent shall be made fat" (Prov. 13:4).

(a) One thing essential to growth in grace is *diligence in the use of private means of grace.* By these I understand such means as a man must use by himself alone, and no one can use for him. I include under this head private prayer, private reading of the Scriptures, and private meditation and self-examination. The man who does not take pains about these three things must never expect to grow. Here are the roots of true Christianity. Wrong here, a man is wrong all the way through! Here is the whole reason that many professing Christians never seem to get on. They are careless and slovenly about their private prayers. They read their Bibles but little, and with very little heartiness of spirit. They give themselves no time for self-inquiry and quiet thought about the state of their souls.

It is useless to conceal from ourselves that the age we live in is full of peculiar dangers. It is an age of great activity, and of much hurry, bustle, and excitement in religion. Many are "running to and fro," no doubt, and "knowledge is increased" (Dan. 12:4). Thousands are ready enough for public meetings, sermon hearing, or anything else in which there is "sensation." Few appear to remember the absolute necessity of making time to "commune with our hearts, and be still" (Ps. 4:4). But without this there is seldom any deep spiritual prosperity. I suspect that

English Christians two hundred years ago read their Bibles more, and were more frequently alone with God, than they are in the present day. Let us remember this point! Private religion must receive our first attention, if we wish our souls to grow.

(b) Another thing that is essential to growth in grace is *carefulness in the use of public means of grace.* By these I understand such means as a man has within his reach as a member of Christ's visible church. Under this head I include the ordinances of regular Sunday worship, the uniting with God's people in common prayer and praise, the preaching of the Word, and the sacrament of the Lord's Supper. I firmly believe that the manner in which these public means of grace are used has much to say to the prosperity of a believer's soul. It is easy to use them in a cold and heartless way. The very familiarity of them is apt to make us careless. The regular return of the same voice, and the same kind of words, and the same ceremonies, is likely to make us sleepy, and callous, and unfeeling. Here is a snare into which too many professing Christians fall. If we would grow, we must be on our guard here. Here is a matter in which the Spirit is often grieved and saints take great damage. Let us strive to use the old prayers, and sing the old hymns, and kneel at the old communion rail, and hear the old truths preached, with as much freshness and appetite as in the year we first believed. It is a sign of bad health when a person loses relish for his food; and it is a sign of spiritual decline when we lose our appetite for means of grace. Whatever we do about public means, let us always do it "with our might" (Eccl.

9:10). This is the way to grow!

(c) Another thing essential to growth in grace is *watchfulness over our conduct in the little matters of everyday life.* Our tempers, our tongues, the discharge of our several relations of life, our employment of time—each and all must be vigilantly attended to if we wish our souls to prosper. Life is made up of days, and days of hours, and the little things of every hour are never so little as to be beneath the care of a Christian. When a tree begins to decay at root or heart, the mischief is first seen at the extreme end of the little branches. "He that despiseth little things," says an uninspired writer, "shall fall by little and little." That witness is true. Let others despise us, if they like, and call us precise and overcareful. Let us patiently hold on our way, remembering that "we serve a precise God," that our Lord's example is to be copied in the least things as well as the greatest, and that we must "take up our cross daily" and hourly, rather than sin. We must aim to have a Christianity that, like the sap of a tree, runs through every twig and leaf of our character, and sanctifies all. This is one way to grow!

(d) Another thing that is essential to growth in grace is *caution about the company we keep and the friendships we form.* Nothing perhaps affects a man's character more than the company he keeps. We catch the ways and tone of those we live and talk with, and unhappily get harm far more easily than good. Disease is infectious, but health is not. Now if a professing Christian deliberately chooses to be intimate with those who are not friends of God and who cling to the world, his soul is sure to take harm. It is hard enough to serve Christ under any circumstances in such a world as this. But it is doubly hard to do it if we are friends of the thoughtless and ungodly. Mistakes in friendship or marriage-engagements are the whole reason that some have entirely ceased to grow. "Evil communications corrupt good manners." "The friendship of the world is enmity with God" (1 Cor. 15:33; James 4:4). Let us seek friends who will stir us up about our prayers, our Bible reading, and our employment of time—about our souls, our salvation, and a world to come. Who can tell the good that a friend's word in season may do, or the harm that it may stop? This is one way to grow.[8]

(e) There is one more thing that is absolutely essential to growth in grace—and that is *regular and habitual communion with the Lord Jesus.* In saying this, let no one suppose for a minute that I am referring to the Lord's Supper. I mean nothing of the kind. I mean that daily habit of intercourse between the believer and his Savior, which can only be carried on by faith, prayer, and meditation. It is a habit, I fear, of which many believers know little. A man may be a believer and have his feet on the rock, and yet live far below his privileges. It is possible to have "union" with Christ, and yet to have little if any "communion" with Him. But, for all that, there is such a thing.

The names and offices of Christ, as laid down in Scripture, appear to me to show unmistakably that this "communion" between the saint and his Savior is not a mere fancy, but a real true thing. Between the "Bridegroom" and His bride—between the "Head" and His members—between the "Physician" and His patients—between the "Advocate" and His clients—between the "Shepherd" and His sheep—between the "Master" and His scholars there is evidently implied a habit of familiar intercourse, of daily application for things needed, of daily pouring out and unburdening our hearts and minds. Such a habit of dealing with Christ is clearly something more than a vague general trust in the work that Christ did for sinners. It is getting *close* to Him, and laying hold on Him with confidence, as a loving, personal Friend. This is what I mean by communion.

Now I believe that no man will ever grow in grace who does not know something experimentally of the habit of "communion." We must not be content with a general orthodox knowledge that justification is by faith and not by works, and that we put our trust in Christ. We must go further than this. We must seek to have personal intimacy with the Lord Jesus, and to deal with Him as a man deals with a loving friend. We must realize what it is to turn to Him first in every need, to talk to Him about every difficulty, to consult Him about every step, to spread before Him all our sorrows, to get Him to share in all our joys, to do all as in His sight, and to go through every day leaning on and looking to Him. This is the way that St. Paul lived: "The life which I now live in the flesh I live by the faith of the Son of God." "To me to live is Christ" (Gal. 2:20; Phil. 1:21). It is ignorance of this way of living that makes so many see no beauty in the book of

Canticles [Song of Solomon]. But it is the man who lives in this way, who keeps up constant communion with Christ—this is the man, I say emphatically, whose soul will grow.

I leave the subject of growth in grace here. Far more might be said about it, if time permitted. But I have said enough, I hope, to convince my readers that the subject is one of vast importance. Let me wind up all with some practical applications.

(1) This book may fall into the hands of some who *know nothing whatever about growth in grace.* They have little or no concern about religion. A little proper Sunday churchgoing or chapel going makes up the sum and substance of their Christianity. They are without spiritual life, and of course they cannot at present grow. Are you one of these people? If you are, you are in a pitiable condition.

Years are slipping away and time is flying. Graveyards are filling up and families are thinning. Death and judgment are getting nearer to us all. And yet you live like one asleep about your soul! What madness! What folly! What suicide can be worse than this?

Awake before it be too late; awake, and arise from the dead, and live to God. Turn to Him who is sitting at the right hand of God, to be your Savior and Friend. Turn to Christ, and cry mightily to Him about your soul. There is yet hope! He who called Lazarus from the grave is not changed. He who commanded the widow's son at Nain to arise from his bier can do miracles yet for your soul. Seek Him at once: seek Christ, if you would not be lost forever. Do not stand still talking, and meaning, and intending, and wishing, and hoping. Seek Christ that you may live, and that living you may grow.

(2) This book may fall into the hands of some who *ought to know something of growth in grace,* but at present know nothing at all. They have made little or no progress since they were first converted. They seem to have "settled on their lees" (Zeph. 1:12). They go on from year to year content with old grace, old experience, old knowledge, old faith, old measure of attainment, old religious expressions, old set phrases. Like the Gibeonites, their bread is always moldy, and their shoes are patched and ragged. They never appear to get on. Are you one of these people? If you are, you are living far below your privileges and responsibilities. It is high time to examine yourself.

If you have reason to hope that you are a true believer and yet do not grow in grace, there must be a fault, and a serious fault somewhere. It cannot be the will of God that your soul should stand still. "He giveth more grace." He "takes pleasure in the prosperity of his servants" (James 4:6; Ps. 35:27). It cannot be for your own happiness or usefulness that your soul should stand still. Without growth you will never rejoice in the Lord (Phil. 4:4). Without growth you will never do good to others. Surely this want of growth is a serious matter! It should raise in you great searchings of heart. There must be some "secret thing" (Job 15:11). There must be some cause.

Take the advice I give you. Resolve this very day that you will find out the reason of your standstill condition. Probe with a faithful and firm hand every corner of your soul. Search from one end of the camp to the other, till you find out the Achan who is weakening your hands. Begin with an application to the Lord Jesus Christ, the great Physician of souls, and ask Him to heal the secret ailment within you, whatever it may be. Begin as if you had never applied to Him before, and ask for grace to cut off the right hand and pluck out the right eye. But never, never be content, if your soul does not grow. For your peace's sake, for your usefulness's sake, for the honor of your Maker's cause, resolve to find out the reason why.

(3) This book may fall into the hands of some who are *really growing in grace*, but are not aware of it, and will not admit it. Their very growth is the reason that they do not see their growth! Their continual increase in humility prevents them feeling that they get on.[9] Like Moses, when he came down from the mount from communing with God, their faces shine. And yet, like Moses, they are not aware of it (Exod. 34:29). Such Christians, I grant freely, are not common. But here and there such are to be found. Like angels' visits, they are few and far between. Happy is the neighborhood where such growing Christians live! To meet them and see them and be in their company is like meeting and seeing a bit of "heaven upon earth."

Now what shall I say to such people? What can I say? What ought I to say? Shall I bid them awake to a consciousness of their growth and be pleased with it? I will do nothing of the kind. Shall I tell them to plume themselves on their own attainments, and look at their own superiority to others? God forbid! I will do nothing of the kind. To tell them such things would do them no good. To tell them such things, above all, would be useless waste of time. If there is any one feature about a growing soul that specially marks him, it is his deep sense of his own unworthiness. He never sees anything to be praised in himself. He only feels that he is an unprofitable servant and the chief of sinners. It is the righteous, in the picture of the judgment day, who say, "Lord, when saw we thee an hungered, and fed thee?" (Matt. 25:37). Extremes do indeed meet strangely sometimes. The conscience-hardened sinner and the eminent saint are in one respect singularly alike. Neither of them fully realizes his own condition. The one does not see his own sin, nor the other his own grace!

But shall I say nothing to growing Christians? Is there no word of counsel I can address to them? The sum and substance of all that I can say is to be found in two sentences: "Go forward!" "Go on!"

We can never have too much humility, too much faith in Christ, too much holiness, too much spirituality of mind, too much charity, too much zeal in doing good to others. Then let us be continually forgetting the things behind, and reaching forth unto the things before (Phil. 3:13). The best of Christians in these matters is infinitely below the perfect pattern of his Lord. Whatever the world may please to say, we may be sure there is no danger of any of us becoming "too good."

Let us cast to the winds as idle talk the common notion that it is possible to be "extreme" and go "too far" in religion. This is a favorite lie of the devil, and one that he circulates with vast industry. No doubt there are enthusiasts and fanatics to be found who bring evil report upon Christianity by their extravagances and follies. But if anyone means to say that a mortal man can be too humble, too charitable, too holy, or too diligent in doing good, he must either be an atheist or a fool. In serving pleasure and money, it is easy to go too far. But in following the things that make up true religion, and in serving Christ, there can be no extreme.

Let us never measure our religion by that of others, and think we are doing enough if we have gone beyond our neighbors. This is another snare of the devil. Let us mind our own business. "What is that to thee?" said our Master on a certain occasion: "Follow thou me" (John 21:22). Let us follow on, aiming at nothing short of perfection. Let us follow on, making Christ's life and character our only pattern and example. Let us follow on, remembering daily that at our best we are miserable sinners. Let us follow on, and never forget that it signifies nothing whether we are better than others or not. At our very best we are far worse than we ought to be. There will always be room for improvement in us. We shall be debtors to Christ's mercy and grace to the very last. Then let us leave off looking at others and comparing ourselves with others. We shall find enough to do if we look at our own hearts.

Last, but not least, if we know anything of growth in grace, and desire to know more, let us not be surprised if we have to go through much trial and affliction in this world. I firmly believe it is the experience of nearly all the most eminent saints. Like their blessed Master, they have been "men of sorrows, acquainted with grief" and "perfected through sufferings" (Isa. 53:3; Heb. 2:10). It is a striking saying of our Lord, "Every branch in me that beareth fruit, my Father purgeth it, that it may bring forth more fruit" (John 15:2). It is a melancholy fact, that constant temporal prosperity, as a general rule, is injurious to a believer's soul. We cannot stand it. Sickness, and losses, and crosses, and anxieties, and disappointments seem absolutely needful to keep us humble, watchful, and spiritual minded. They are as needful as the pruning knife to the vine, and the refiner's furnace to the gold. They are not pleasant to flesh and blood. We do not like them, and often do not see their meaning. "No chastening for the present seemeth to be joyous, but grievous: nevertheless, afterward, it yieldeth the peaceable fruit of righteousness" (Heb. 12:11). We shall find that all worked for our good when we reach heaven. Let these thoughts abide in our minds, if we love growth in grace. When days of darkness come upon us, let us not count it a strange thing. Rather let us remember that lessons are learned on such days that would never have been learned in sunshine. Let us say to ourselves, "This also is for my profit, that I may be a partaker of God's holiness. It is sent in love. I am in God's best school. Correction is instruction. This is meant to make me grow."

I leave the subject of growth in grace here. I trust I have said

enough to set some readers thinking about it. All things are growing older: the world is growing old; we ourselves are growing
older. A few more summers, a few more winters, a few more sick-
nesses, a few more sorrows, a few more weddings, a few more
funerals, a few more meetings, and a few more partings, and
then—what? Why the grass will be growing over our graves!

Now would it not be well to look within, and put to our
souls a simple question? In religion, in the things that concern
our peace, in the great matter of personal holiness, are we getting
on?

1. "True grace is progressive, of a spreading, growing nature. It is with grace as it is
   with light: first, there is the daybreak; then it shines brighter to the full noonday.
   The saints are not only compared to stars for their light, but to trees for their
   growth (Isa. 61:3; Hos. 14:5). A good Christian is not like Hezekiah's sun that
   went backwards, nor Joshua's sun that stood still, but is always advancing in holiness, and increasing with the increase of God." (Thomas Watson, minister of St.
   Stephen's Walbrook, *A Body of Divinity*, 1660.)

2. "The growth of grace is the best evidence of the truth of grace. Things that have
   not life will not grow. A picture will not grow. A stake in a hedge will not grow.
   But a plant that hath vegetative life will grow. The growing of grace shows it to
   be alive in the soul." (T. Watson, 1660.)

3. "Christian, as ever you would stir up others to exalt the God of grace, look to the
   exercise and improvement of our own graces. When poor servants live in a family,
   and see the faith, and love, and wisdom, and patience, and humility of a master,
   shining like the stars in heaven, it draws forth their hearts to bless the Lord that
   ever they came into such a family. . . . When men's graces shine as Moses' face did,
   when their life, as one speaketh of Joseph's life, is a very heaven, sparkling with
   virtues as so many bright stars, how much others are stirred up to glorify God, and
   cry, 'These are Christians indeed! These are an honor to their God, a crown to their
   Christ, and a credit to their gospel! Oh, if they were all such, we would be
   Christians too!'" (Thomas Brooks, *Unsearchable Riches*, 1661.)

4. "The right manner of growth is to grow less in one's own eyes. 'I am a worm and no

man' (Ps. 22:6). The sight of corruption and ignorance makes a Christian grow into a dislike of himself. He doth vanish in his own eyes. Job abhorred himself in the dust (Job 42:6). This is good, to grow out of conceit with oneself." (T. Watson, 1660.)

5. "It is a sign of not growing in grace, when we are less troubled about sin. Time was when the least sin did grieve us (as the least hair makes the eye weep), but now we can digest sin without remorse. Time was when a Christian was troubled if he neglected closet prayer; now he can omit family prayer. Time was when vain thoughts did not trouble him; now he is not troubled for loose practices. There is a sad declension in religion; and grace is so far from growing that we can hardly perceive its pulse to beat." (T. Watson, 1660.)

6. "If now you would be rich in graces, look to your walking. It is not the knowing soul, nor the talking soul, but the close-walking soul, the obedient soul, that is rich. Others may be rich in notions, but none so rich in spiritual experience, and in all holy and heavenly graces, as close-walking Christians." (Thomas Brooks, 1661.)

It is a sign of not growing in grace, when we grow more worldly. Perhaps once we were mounted into higher orbits, we did set our hearts on things above, and speak the language of Canaan. But now our minds are taken off heaven, we dig our comforts out of these lower mines, and with Satan compass the earth. It is a sign we are going downhill apace, and our grace is in a consumption. It is observable when nature decays, and people are near dying, they grow more stooping. And truly when men's hearts grow more stooping to the earth, and they can hardly lift up themselves to an heavenly thought, if grace be not dead, yet it is ready to die." (T. Watson, 1660.)

7. "Experience will tell every Christian that the more strictly, and closely, and constantly he walketh with God, the stronger he groweth in duty. Infused habits are advantaged by exercise. As the fire that kindled the wood for sacrifices upon the altar first came down from heaven, but then was to be kept alive by the care and labor of the priests, so the habits of spiritual grace are indeed infused from God, and must be maintained by daily influences from God, yet with a concurrence also of our own labors, in waiting upon God, and exercising ourselves with godliness; and the more a Christian doth so exercise himself, the more strong he shall grow." (Collinges, on "Providence," 1678.)

8. "Let them be thy choicest companions, that have made Christ their chiefest companion. Do not so much eye the outsides of men as their inside: look most to their internal worth. Many persons have their eyes upon the external garb of a professor. But give me a Christian that minds the internal worth of persons, that makes such as are most filled with the fullness of God his choicest and chiefest companions." (T. Brooks, 1661.)

9. "Christians may be growing when they think they do not grow. 'There is that maketh himself poor, yet he is rich' (Prov. 13:7). The sight that Christians have of their defects in grace, and their thirst after greater measures of grace, makes them think they do not grow. He who covets a great estate, because he hath not so much as he desires, thinks himself poor." (T. Watson, 1660.)

"Souls may be rich in grace, and yet not know it, not perceive it. The child is heir to a crown or a great estate, but knows it not. Moses' face did shine, and others saw it, but he perceived it not. So many a precious soul is rich in grace, and others see it, and know it, and bless God for it, and yet the poor soul perceives it not. Sometimes this arises from the soul's strong desires of spiritual riches. The strength of the soul's desires after spiritual riches doth often take away the very sense of growing spiritually rich. Many covetous men's desires are so strongly carried forth after earthly riches, that though they do grow rich, yet they cannot perceive it, they cannot believe it. It is just so with many a precious Christian: his desires after spiritual riches are so strong, that they take away the very sense of his growing rich in spirituals. Many Christian have much worth within them, but they see it not. It was a good man that said, 'The Lord was in this place and I knew it not.' Again, this ariseth sometimes from men neglecting to cast up their accounts. Many men thrive and grow rich, and yet, by neglecting to cast up their accounts, they cannot tell whether they go forward or backward. It is so with many precious souls. Again, this ariseth sometimes from the soul's too frequent casting up of its accounts. If a man should cast up his accounts once a week, or once a month, he may not be able to discern that he doth grow rich, and yet he may grow rich. But let him compare one year with another, and he shall clearly see that he doth grow rich. Again, this sometimes ariseth from the soul's mistakes in casting up its accounts. The soul many times mistakes: it is in a hurry, and then it puts down ten for a hundred, and a hundred for a thousand. Look, as hypocrites put down their counters for gold, their pence for pounds, and always prize themselves above the market, so sincere souls do often put down their pounds for pence, their thousands for hundreds, and still prize themselves below the market." (T. Brooks, *Unsearchable Riches*, 1661.)

THE RULER
OF THE WAVES

∾

"AND THERE AROSE A GREAT STORM OF WIND, AND THE WAVES BEAT INTO
THE SHIP, SO THAT IT WAS NOW FULL. AND HE WAS IN THE HINDER PART
OF THE SHIP, ASLEEP ON A PILLOW: AND THEY AWAKE HIM, AND SAY UNTO
HIM, MASTER, CAREST THOU NOT THAT WE PERISH? AND HE AROSE, AND
REBUKED THE WIND, AND SAID UNTO THE SEA, PEACE, BE STILL. AND THE
WIND CEASED, AND THERE WAS A GREAT CALM. AND HE SAID UNTO THEM,
WHY ARE YE SO FEARFUL? HOW IS IT THAT YE HAVE NO FAITH?"
(Mark 4:37–40)

IT WOULD BE WELL if professing Christians in modern days studied the four Gospels more than they do. No doubt all Scripture is profitable. It is not wise to exalt one part of the Bible at the expense of another. But I think it should be good for some who are very familiar with the Epistles, if they knew a little more about Matthew, Mark, Luke, and John.

Now why do I say this? I say it because I want professing Christians to know more about Christ. It is well to be acquainted with all the doctrines and principles of Christianity. It is better to be acquainted with Christ Himself. It is well to be familiar with faith, and grace, and justification, and sanctification. They are all matters "pertaining to the King." But it is far better to be familiar with Jesus Himself, to see the King's own face, and to behold His beauty. This is one secret of eminent holiness. He who would be conformed to Christ's image, and become a Christlike man, must be constantly studying Christ Himself.

Now the Gospels were written to make us acquainted with Christ. The Holy Ghost has told us the story of His life and death—His sayings and His doings, four times over. Four different, inspired hands have drawn the picture of the Savior. His ways, His manners, His feelings, His wisdom, His grace, His patience, His love, His power, are graciously unfolded to us by four different witnesses. Ought not the sheep to be familiar with the Shepherd? Ought not the patient to be familiar with the Physician? Ought not the bride to be familiar with the Bridegroom? Ought not the sinner to be familiar with the Savior? Beyond doubt it ought to be so. The Gospels were written to make men familiar with Christ, and therefore I wish men to study the Gospels.

On whom must we build our souls if we would be accepted with God? We must build on *the rock*, Christ. From whom must we draw that grace of the Spirit, which we daily need in order to be fruitful? We must draw from *the vine, Christ*. To whom must we look for sympathy when earthly friends fail us or die? We must look to our elder *brother, Christ*. By whom must our prayers be presented, if they are to be heard on high? They must be presented by our *advocate*, Christ. With whom do we hope to spend the thousand years of glory, and the after eternity? With the *King of kings, Christ.* Surely we cannot know this Christ too well! Surely there is not a word, nor a deed, nor a day, nor a step, nor a thought in the record of His life, which ought not to be precious to us. We should labor to be familiar with every line that is written about Jesus.

Come now, and let us study a page in our Master's history. Let us consider what we may learn from the verses of Scripture that stand at the head of this chapter. You there see Jesus crossing the lake of Galilee, in a boat with His disciples. You see a sudden storm arise while He is asleep. The waves beat into the boat and fill it. Death seems to be close at hand. The frightened disciples awake their Master and cry for help. He arises and rebukes the wind and the waves, and at once there is a calm. He mildly reproves the faithless fears of His companions, and all is over. Such is the picture. It is one full of deep instruction. Come now, and let us examine what we are meant to learn.

I. Let us learn, first of all, that *following Christ will not prevent our having earthly sorrows and troubles.*

Here are the chosen disciples of the Lord Jesus in great anxiety. The faithful little flock that believed when priests, and scribes, and Pharisees were all alike unbelieving, is allowed by the Shepherd to be much disquieted. The fear of death breaks in upon them like an armed man. The deep water seems likely to go over their souls. Peter, James, and John, the pillars of the Church about to be planted in the world, are much distressed.

Perhaps they had not reckoned on all this. Perhaps they had expected that Christ's service would at any rate lift them above the reach of earthly trials. Perhaps they thought that He who could raise the dead, and heal the sick, and feed multitudes with a few loaves, and cast out devils with a word—He would never allow His servants to be sufferers upon earth. Perhaps they had supposed He would always grant them smooth journeys, fine weather, an easy course, and freedom from trouble and care.

If the disciples thought so, they were much mistaken. The Lord Jesus taught them that a man may be one of His chosen servants, and yet have to go through many an anxiety, and endure many a pain.

It is good to understand this clearly. It is good to understand that Christ's service never did secure a man from all the ills that flesh is heir to, and never will. If you are a believer, you must reckon on having your share of sickness and pain, of sorrow and tears, of losses and crosses, of deaths and bereavements, of partings and separations, of vexations and disappointments, so long as you are in the body. Christ never undertakes that you shall get to heaven without these. He has undertaken that all who come to Him shall have all things pertaining to life and godliness; but He has never undertaken that He will make them prosperous, or rich, or healthy, and that death and sorrow shall never come to their family.

I have the privilege of being one of Christ's ambassadors. In His name I can offer eternal life to any man, woman, or child who is willing to have it. In His name I do offer pardon, peace, grace, glory, to any son or daughter of Adam who reads this book. But I dare not offer that person worldly prosperity as a part and parcel of the Gospel. I dare not offer him long life, an increased income, and freedom from pain. I dare not promise the man who takes up the cross and follows Christ, that in the following he shall never meet with a storm.

I know well that many do not like these terms. They would prefer having Christ and good health—Christ and plenty of money —Christ and no deaths in their family—Christ and no wearing cares—Christ and a perpetual morning without clouds. But they do not like Christ and the cross—Christ and tribulation—Christ and the conflict—Christ and the howling wind—Christ and the storm.

Is this the secret thought of anyone who is reading this chapter? Believe me, if it is, you are very wrong. Listen to me, and I will try to show you have yet much to learn.

How should you know who are true Christians, if following Christ was the way to be free from trouble? How should we discern the wheat from the chaff, if it were not for the winnowing of trial? How should we know whether men served Christ for His own sake or from selfish motives, if His service brought health and wealth with it as a matter of course? The winds of winter soon show us which of the trees are evergreen and which are not.

The storms of affliction and care are useful in the same way. They discover whose faith is real, and whose is nothing but profession and form.

How would the great work of sanctification go on in a man if he had no trial? Trouble is often the only fire that will burn away the dross that clings to our hearts. Trouble is the pruning-knife that the great Husbandman employs in order to make us fruitful in good works. The harvest of the Lord's field is seldom ripened by sunshine only. It must go through its days of wind, and rain, and storm.

If you desire to serve Christ and be saved, I entreat you to take the Lord on His own terms. Make up your mind to meet with your share of crosses and sorrows, and then you will not be surprised. For want of understanding this, many seem to run well for a season, and then turn back in disgust, and are cast away.

If you profess to be a child of God, leave to the Lord Jesus to sanctify you in His own way. Rest satisfied that He never makes any mistakes. Be sure that He does all things well. The winds may howl around you, and the waters swell. But fear not, "He is leading you by the right way, that He may bring you to a city of habitation" (Psalm 107:7).

II. Let us learn, in the second place, that the Lord *Jesus Christ is truly and really Man.*

There are words used in this little history that, like many other passages in the Gospel, bring out this truth in a very striking way. We are told that when the waves began to break on the ship, Jesus was in the hinder part, "asleep on a pillow." He was weary; and who can wonder at it, after reading the account given in the fourth chapter of Mark? After laboring all day to do good to souls—after preaching in the open air to vast multitudes, Jesus was fatigued. Surely if the sleep of the laboring man is sweet, much more sweet must have been the sleep of our blessed Lord!

Let us settle in our minds this great truth, that Jesus Christ was verily and indeed Man. He was equal to the Father in all things, and the eternal God. But He was also Man, and took part of flesh and blood, and was made like unto us in all things, sin only excepted. He had a body like our own. Like us, He was born of a woman. Like us, He grew and increased in stature. Like us, He was often hungry and thirsty, and faint and weary. Like us, He ate and drank, rested and slept. Like us, He sorrowed, and wept, and felt. It is all very wonderful, but so it is. He who made the heavens went to and fro as a poor, weary Man on earth! He who ruled over principalities and powers in heavenly places, took on Him a frail body like our own. He who might have dwelt forever in the glory that He had with the Father, amidst the praises of legions of angels, came down to earth and dwelt as a Man among sinful men. Surely this fact alone is an amazing miracle of condescension, grace, pity, and love.

I find a deep mine of comfort in this thought, that Jesus is perfect Man no less than perfect God. He in whom I am told by Scripture to trust is not only a great High Priest, but a feeling High Priest. He is not only a powerful Savior, but a sympathizing

Savior. He is not only the Son of God, mighty to save, but the Son of man, able to feel.

Who does not know that sympathy is one of the sweetest things left to us in this sinful world? It is one of the bright seasons in our dark journey here below, when we can find a person who enters into our troubles, and goes along with us in our anxieties —who can weep when we weep, and rejoice when we rejoice.

Sympathy is far better than money, and far rarer too. Thousands can give who know not what it is to feel. Sympathy has the greatest power to draw us and to open our hearts. Proper and correct counsel often falls dead and useless on a heavy heart. Cold advice often makes us shut up, shrink, and withdraw into ourselves, when tendered in the day of trouble. But genuine sympathy in such a day will call out all our better feelings, if we have any, and obtain an influence over us when nothing else can. Give me the friend who, though poor in gold and silver, has always ready a sympathizing heart.

Our God knows all this well. He knows the very secrets of man's heart. He knows the ways by which that heart is most easily approached, and the springs by which that heart is most readily moved. He has wisely provided that the Savior of the Gospel should be feeling as well as mighty. He has given us one who has not only a strong hand to pluck us as brands from the burning, but a sympathizing heart on which the laboring and heavy-laden may find rest.

I see a marvelous proof of love and wisdom in the union of

two natures in Christ's person. It was marvelous love in our Savior to condescend to go through weakness and humiliation for our sakes, ungodly rebels as we are. It was marvelous wisdom to fit Himself in this way to be the very Friend of friends, who could not only save man, but meet him on his own ground. I want one able to perform all things needful to redeem my soul. This Jesus can do, for He is the eternal Son of God. I want one able to understand my weakness and infirmities, and to deal gently with my soul, while tied to a body of death. This again Jesus can do, for He was the Son of man, and had flesh and blood like my own. Had my Savior been God only, I might perhaps have trusted Him, but I never could have come near to Him without fear. Had my Savior been Man only, I might have loved Him, but I never could have felt sure that He was able to take away my sins. But, blessed be God, my Savior is God as well as Man, and Man as well as God— God, and so able to deliver me—Man, and so able to feel with me. Almighty power and deepest sympathy are met together in one glorious person, Jesus Christ, my Lord. Surely a believer in Christ has a strong consolation. He may well trust, and not be afraid.

If any reader of this chapter knows what it is to go to the throne of grace for mercy and pardon, let him never forget that the Mediator by whom he draws near to God is the Man Christ Jesus.

Your soul's business is in the hand of a High Priest who can be touched with the feeling of your infirmities. You have not to do with a being of so high and glorious a nature that your mind can in no wise comprehend Him. You have to do with Jesus, who had a body like your own and was a Man upon earth like yourself. He well knows that world through which you are struggling, for He dwelt in the midst of it thirty-three years. He well knows "the contradictions of sinners," which so often discourages you, for He endured it Himself (Heb. 12:3). He well knows the art and cunning of your spiritual enemy, the devil, for He wrestled with him in the wilderness. Surely, with such an advocate you may well feel bold.

If you know what it is to apply to the Lord Jesus for spiritual comfort in earthly troubles, you should well remember the days of His flesh, and His human nature.

You are applying to One who knows your feelings by experience, and has drunk deep of the bitter cup, for He was "a Man of sorrows, and acquainted with grief" (Isa. 53:3). Jesus knows the heart of a man—the bodily pains of a man—the difficulties of a man, for he was a Man Himself, and had flesh and blood upon earth. He sat wearied by the well at Sychar. He wept over the grave of Lazarus at Bethany. He sweat great drops of blood at Gethsemane. He groaned with anguish at Calvary.

He is no stranger to your sensations. He is acquainted with everything that belongs to human nature, sin only excepted.

(a) Are you poor and needy? So also was Jesus. The foxes had holes, and the birds of the air had nests, but the Son of man had nowhere to lay His head. He dwelt in a despised city. Men used to say, "Can any good thing come out of Nazareth?" (John 1:46).

He was esteemed a carpenter's son. He preached in a borrowed boat, rode into Jerusalem on a borrowed donkey, and was buried in a borrowed tomb.

(b) Are you alone in the world, and neglected by those who ought to love you? So also was Jesus. He came unto His own, and they received Him not. He came to be a Messiah to the lost sheep of the house of Israel, and they rejected Him. The princes of this world would not acknowledge Him. The few who followed Him were publicans and fishermen. And even these at the last forsook Him, and were scattered every man to his own place.

(c) Are you misunderstood, misrepresented, slandered, and persecuted? So also was Jesus. He was called a glutton and a wine-bibber, a friend of publicans, a Samaritan, a madman, and a devil. His character was belied. False charges were laid against Him. An unjust sentence was passed upon Him, and, though innocent, He was condemned as a malefactor, and as such died on the cross.

(d) Does Satan tempt you, and offer horrid suggestions to your mind? So also did he tempt Jesus. He bade Him to distrust God's fatherly providence. "Command these stones to be made bread." He proposed to Him to tempt God by exposing Himself to unnecessary danger. "Cast thyself down" from the pinnacle of the temple. He suggested to Him to obtain the kingdoms of the world for His own, by one little act of submission to himself. "All these things will I give thee, if thou wilt fall down and worship me" (Matt. 4:1–10).

(e) Do you ever feel great agony and conflict of mind? Do you feel in darkness as if God had left you? So did Jesus. Who can tell the extent of the sufferings of mind He went through in the garden? Who can measure the depth of His soul's pain when He cried, "My God! my God! why hast thou forsaken me" (Matt. 27:46)?

It is impossible to conceive a Savior more suited to the wants of man's heart than our Lord Jesus Christ—suited not only by His power, but by His sympathy—suited not only by His divinity, but by His humanity. Labor, I beseech you, to get firmly impressed on your mind that Christ, the refuge of souls, is Man as well as God. Honor Him as King of kings, and Lord of lords. But while you do this, never forget that He had a body and was a Man. Grasp this truth and never let it go. The unhappy Socinian errs fearfully when he says that Christ was only Man, and not God. But let not the rebound from that error make you forget that while Christ was very God He was also very Man.

Listen not for a moment to the wretched argument of the Roman Catholic when he tells you that the Virgin Mary and the saints are more sympathizing than Christ. Answer him that such an argument springs from ignorance of the Scriptures and of Christ's true nature. Answer him, that you have not so learned Christ as to regard Him only as an austere Judge and a being to be feared. Answer him, that the four Gospels have taught you to regard Him as the most loving and sympathizing of friends, as well as the mightiest and most powerful of Saviors. Answer him, that you want no comfort from saints and angels, from the Virgin

Mary or from Gabriel, so long as you can repose your weary soul on THE MAN CHRIST JESUS.

III. Let us learn, in the third place, *that there may be much weakness and infirmity, even in a true Christian.*

You have a striking proof of this in the conduct of the disciples here recorded, when the waves broke over the ship. They awoke Jesus in haste. They said to Him, in fear and anxiety, "Master, carest thou not that we perish?"

There was *impatience*. They might have waited till their Lord thought fit to arise from His sleep.

There was *unbelief*. They forgot that they were in the keeping of One who had all power in His hand. "We perish."

There was *distrust*. They spoke as if they doubted their Lord's care and thoughtfulness for their safety and well-being. "Carest thou not that we perish?"

Poor faithless men! What business had they to be afraid? They had seen proof upon proof that all must be well so long as the Bridegroom was with them. They had witnessed repeated examples of His love and kindness towards them, sufficient to convince them that He would never let them come to real harm. But all was forgotten in the present danger. Sense of immediate peril often makes men have a bad memory. Fear is often unable to reason from past experience. They heard the winds. They saw the waves. They felt the cold waters beating over them. They fancied death was close at hand. They could wait no longer in suspense. "Carest thou not," said they, "that we perish?"

But, after all, let us understand this is only a picture of what is constantly going on among believers in every age. There are too many disciples, I suspect, at this very day, like those who are here described.

Many of God's children get on very well so long as they have no trials. They follow Christ very tolerably in the time of fair weather. They fancy they are trusting Him entirely. They flatter themselves they have cast every care on Him. They obtain the reputation of being very good Christians.

But suddenly some unlooked-for trial assails them. Their property makes itself wings and flies away. Their own health fails. Death comes up into their house. Tribulation or persecution ariseth, because of the word. And where now is their faith? Where is the strong confidence they thought they had? Where is their peace, their hope, their resignation? Alas, they are sought for and not found. They are weighed in the balances and found wanting. Fear, and doubt, and distress, and anxiety break in upon them like a flood, and they seem at their wits' end. I know that this is a sad description. I only put it to the conscience of every real Christian, whether it is not correct and true.

The plain truth is that there is no literal and absolute perfection among true Christians, so long as they are in the body. The best and brightest of God's saints is but a poor mixed being. Converted, renewed, and sanctified though he be, he is still compassed with infirmity. There is not a just man upon earth that always doeth good and sinneth not. In many things we offend all.

A man may have true saving faith, and yet not have it always close at hand, and ready to be used (Eccles. 7:20; James 3:2).

Abraham was the father of the faithful. By faith he forsook his country and his kindred, and went out according to the command of God, to a land he had never seen. By faith he was content to dwell in the land as a stranger, believing that God would give it to him for an inheritance. And yet this very Abraham was so far overcome by unbelief, that he allowed Sarah to be called his sister, and not his wife, through the fear of man. Here was great infirmity. Yet there have been few greater saints than Abraham.

David was a man after God's own heart. He had faith to go out to battle with the giant Goliath when he was but a youth. He publicly declared his belief that the Lord who delivered him from the paw of the lion and bear, would deliver him from this Philistine. He had faith to believe God's promise that he should one day be King of Israel, though he was owned by few followers—though Saul pursued him like a partridge on the mountains and there often seemed but a step between him and death. And yet this very David at one time was so far overtaken by fear and unbelief that he said, "I shall one day perish by the hand of Saul" (1 Sam. 27:1). He forgot the many wonderful deliverances he had experienced at God's hand. He only thought of his present danger, and took refuge among the ungodly Philistines. Surely here was great infirmity. Yet there have been few stronger believers than David.

I know it is easy for a man to reply, "All this is very true, but it does not excuse the fears of the disciples. They had Jesus actually with them. They ought not to have been afraid. I should never have been so cowardly and faithless as they were!" I tell the man who argues in that way, that he knows little of his own heart. I tell him no one knows the length and breadth of his own infirmities if he has not been tempted. No one can say how much weakness might appear in himself if he was placed in circumstances to call it forth.

Does any reader of this book think that he believes in Christ? Do you feel such love and confidence in Him that you cannot understand being greatly moved by any event that could happen? It is all well. I am glad to hear it. But has this faith been tried? Has this confidence been put to the test? If not, take heed of condemning these disciples hastily. Be not high-minded, but fear. Think not because your heart is in a lively frame now, that such a frame will always last. Say not, because your feelings are warm and fervent today, "Tomorrow shall be as today, and much more abundant." Say not, because your heart is lifted up just now with a strong sense of Christ's mercy, "I shall never forget Him as long as I live." Oh, learn to abate something of this flattering estimate of yourself. You do not know yourself thoroughly. There are more things in your inward man than you are at present aware of. The Lord may leave you as He did Hezekiah, to show you all that is in your heart (2 Chron. 32:31). Blessed is he who is "clothed with humility."—"Happy is he that feareth always." "Let him that thinketh he standeth take heed lest he fall" (1 Pet. 5:5; Prov. 28:14; 1 Cor. 10:12).

Why do I dwell on this? Do I want to apologize for the corruptions of professing Christians, and excuse their sins? God forbid! —Do I want to lower the standard of sanctification, and countenance anyone in being a lazy, idle soldier of Christ? God forbid!— Do I want to wipe out the broad line of distinction between the converted and the unconverted, and to wink at inconsistencies? Once more I say, God forbid!—I hold strongly that there is a mighty difference between the true Christian and the false, between the believer and the unbeliever, between the children of God and the children of the world. I hold strongly that this difference is not merely one of faith, but of life—not only one of profession, but of practice. I hold strongly that the ways of the believer should be as distinct from those of the unbeliever, as bitter from sweet, light from darkness, heat from cold.

But I do want young Christians to understand what they must expect to find in *themselves*. I want to prevent their being stumbled and puzzled by the discovery of their own weakness and infirmity. I want them to see that they may have true faith and grace, in spite of all the devil's whispers to the contrary, though they feel within doubts and fears. I want them to observe that Peter, and James, and John, and their brethren were true disciples, and yet not so spiritual but that they could be afraid. I do not tell them to make the unbelief of the disciples an excuse for themselves. But I do tell them that it shows plainly, that so long as they are in the body they must not expect faith to be above the reach of fear.

Above all, I want all Christians to understand what they must expect *in other believers*. You must not hastily conclude that a man has no grace merely because you see in him some corruption. There are spots on the face of the sun; and yet the sun shines brightly and enlightens the whole world. There is quartz and dross mixed up with many a lump of gold that comes from Australia; and yet who thinks the gold on that account worth nothing at all? There are flaws in some of the finest diamonds in the world; and yet they do not prevent their being rated at a priceless value. Away with this morbid squeamishness that makes many ready to excommunicate a man if he only has a few faults! Let us be more quick to see grace and more slow to see imperfections! Let us know that, if we cannot allow there is grace where there is corruption, we shall find no grace in the world. We are yet in the body. The devil is not dead. We are not yet like the angels. Heaven has not yet begun. The leprosy is not out of the walls of the house, however much we may scrape them, and never will be till the house is taken down. Our bodies are indeed the temple of the Holy Ghost, but not a perfect temple until they are raised or changed. Grace is indeed a treasure, but a treasure in earthen vessels. It is possible for a man to forsake all for Christ's sake, and yet to be overtaken occasionally with doubts and fears.

I beseech every reader of this book to remember this. It is a lesson worth attention. The Apostles believed in Christ, loved

Christ, and gave up all to follow Christ. And yet you see in this storm the Apostles were afraid. Learn to be charitable in your judgment of them. Learn to be moderate in your expectations from your own heart. Contend to the death for the truth that no man is a true Christian who is not converted, and is not a holy man. But allow that a man may be converted, have a new heart, and be a holy man, and yet be liable to infirmity, doubts, and fears.

IV. Let us learn, in the fourth place, *the power of the Lord Jesus Christ.*

You have a striking example of His power in the history upon which I am now dwelling. The waves were breaking into the ship where Jesus was. The terrified disciples awoke Him, and cried for help. "He arose and rebuked the wind, and said unto the sea, Peace, be still. And the wind ceased, and there was a great calm." This was a wonderful miracle. No one could do this but One who was almighty.

Make the winds cease with a word! Who does not know that it is a common saying, in order to describe an impossibility, "You might as well speak to the wind!" Yet Jesus rebukes the wind and at once it ceases. This was power.

Calm the waves with a voice! What reader of history does not know that a mighty King of England tried in vain to stop the tide rising on the shore? Yet here is One who says to raging waves in a storm, "Peace, be still," and at once there was a calm. Here was power.

It is good for all men to have clear views of the Lord Jesus Christ's power. Let the sinner know that the merciful Savior to whom he is urged to flee, and in whom he is invited to trust, is nothing less than the Almighty, and has power over all flesh to eternal life (Rev. 1:8; John 17:2). Let the anxious inquirer understand that if he will only venture on Jesus, and take up the cross, he ventures on One who has all power in heaven and earth (Matt. 28:18). Let the believer remember as he journeys through the wilderness, that his Mediator, and Advocate, and Physician, and Shepherd, and Redeemer, is Lord of lords, and King of kings, and that through Him all things may be done (Rev. 17:14; Phil. 4:13). Let all study the subject, for it deserves to be studied.

(a) Study it in His works of creation. "All things were made by Him, and without Him was not any thing made that was made" (John 1:3). The heavens and all their glorious host of inhabitants—the earth and all that it contains—the sea and all that is in it—all creation, from the sun on high to the least worm below, was the work of Christ. He spoke and they came into being. He commanded and they began to exist. That very Jesus, who was born of a poor woman at Bethlehem and lived in a carpenter's house at Nazareth, had been the Former of all things. Was not this power?

(b) Study it in His works of providence, and the orderly continuance of all things in the world. "By Him all things consist" (Col. 1:17). Sun, moon, and stars roll around in a perfect system. Spring, summer, autumn, and winter follow one another in regular order. They continue to this day and fail not, according to the ordinance of Him who died on Calvary (Psalm 119:91). The kingdoms of this world rise and increase, and decline and pass away. The rulers of the earth plan, and scheme, and make laws, and change laws, and war, and pull down one and raise up another. But they little think that they rule only by the will of Jesus and that nothing happens without the permission of the Lamb of God. They do not know that they and their subjects are all as a drop of water in the hand of the crucified One, and that He increases the nations and diminishes the nations, just according to His mind. Is not this power?

(c) Study the subject not least in the miracles worked by our Lord Jesus Christ during the three years of His ministry upon earth. Learn from the mighty works that He did, that the things that are impossible with man are possible with Christ. Regard every one of His miracles as an emblem and figure of spiritual things. See in it a lovely picture of what He is able to do for your soul. He who could raise the dead with a word can just as easily raise man from the death of sin. He who could give sight to the blind, hearing to the deaf, and speech to the dumb, can also make sinners to see the kingdom of God, hear the joyful sound of the Gospel, and speak forth the praise of redeeming love. He who could heal leprosy with a touch, can heal any disease of heart. He who could cast out devils can bid every besetting sin yield to His grace. Oh, begin to read Christ's miracles in this light! Wicked, and bad, and corrupt as you may feel, take comfort in the thought that you are not beyond Christ's power to heal. Remember that in Christ there is not only a fullness of mercy, but a fullness of power.

(d) Study the subject in particular *as placed before you this day*. I dare be sure your heart has sometimes been tossed to and fro like the waves in a storm. You have found it agitated like the waters of the troubled sea when it cannot rest. Come and hear this day that there is One who can give you rest. Jesus can say to your heart, whatever may be its ailment, "Peace, be still!"

What though your conscience within be lashed by the recollection of countless transgressions, and torn by every gust of temptation? What though the remembrance of past hideous profligacy be grievous unto you, and the burden intolerable? What though your heart seems full of evil, and sin appears to drag you whither it will like a slave? What though the devil rides to and fro over your soul like a conqueror, and tells you it is vain to struggle against him, there is no hope for you? I tell you there is One who can give even you pardon and peace. My Lord and Master Jesus Christ can rebuke the devil's raging, can calm even your soul's misery, and say even to you, "Peace, be still!" He can scatter that cloud of guilt that now weighs you down. He can bid despair depart. He can drive fear away. He can remove the spirit of bondage and fill you with the spirit of adoption. Satan may hold your soul like a strong man armed, but Jesus is stronger than he, and when He commands, the prisoners must go free. Oh, if any troubled reader wants a calm within, let him go this day to Jesus Christ and all shall yet be well!

But what if your heart be right with God, and yet you are pressed down with a load of earthly trouble? What if the fear of poverty is tossing you to and fro and seems likely to overwhelm you? What if pain of body be racking you to distraction day after day? What if you are suddenly laid aside from active usefulness, and compelled by infirmity to sit still and do nothing? What if death has come into your home and taken away your Rachel, or Joseph, or Benjamin and left you alone, crushed to the ground with sorrow? What if all this has happened? Still there is comfort in Christ. He can speak peace to wounded hearts as easily as calm troubled seas. He can rebuke rebellious wills as powerfully as raging winds. He can make storms of sorrow abate and silence tumultuous passions as surely as He stopped the Galilean storm. He can say to the heaviest anxiety, "Peace, be still!" The floods of care and tribulation may be mighty, but Jesus sits upon the waterfloods and is mightier than the waves of the sea (Ps. 93:4). The winds of trouble may howl fiercely round you, but Jesus holds them in His hand and can stay them. Oh, if any reader of this book is brokenhearted, and care-worn, and sorrowful, let him go to Jesus Christ and cry to Him, and he shall be refreshed. "Come unto me," He says, "all ye that labor and are heavy laden, and I will give you rest" (Matt. 11:28).

I invite all who profess and call themselves Christians, to take large views of Christ's power. Doubt anything else if you will, but never doubt Christ's power. Whether you do not secretly love sin, may be doubtful. Whether you are not privately clinging to the world, may be doubtful. Whether the pride of your nature is not rising against the idea of being saved as a poor sinner by grace, may be doubtful. But one thing is not doubtful, and that is that Christ is "able to save to the uttermost," and will save you, if you will let Him (Heb. 7:25).

V. Let us learn, in the last place, *how tenderly and patiently the Lord Jesus deals with weak believers.*

We see this truth brought out in His words to His disciples, when the wind ceased and there was a calm. He might well have rebuked them sharply. He might well have reminded them of all the great things He had done for them and reproved them for their cowardice and mistrust. But there is nothing of anger in the Lord's words. He simply asks two questions. "Why are ye so fearful? How is it that ye have no faith?"

The whole of our Lord's conduct towards His disciples on earth deserves close consideration; it throws a beautiful light on the compassion and longsuffering that there is in Him. No master surely ever had scholars so slow to learn their lessons as Jesus had in the Apostles. No scholars surely ever had so patient and forbearing a teacher as the Apostles had in Christ. Gather up all the evidence on this subject that lies scattered through the Gospels, and see the truth of what I say.

At no time of our Lord's ministry did the disciples seem to comprehend fully the object of His coming into the world. The humiliation, the atonement, the crucifixion, were hidden things to them. The plainest words and clearest warnings from their

Master of what was going to befall Him seemed to have had no effect on their minds. They understood not. They perceived not. It was hid from their eyes. Once Peter even tried to dissuade our Lord from suffering. "Be it far from thee, Lord," he said, "this shall not be unto thee" (Matt. 16:22; Luke 18:34; 9:45).

Frequently you will see things in their spirit and demeanor that are not at all to be commended. One day we are told they disputed among themselves who should be greatest (Mark 9:34). Another day they considered not His miracles and their hearts were hardened (Mark 6:52). Once two of them wished to call down fire from heaven upon a village, because it did not receive them (Luke 9:54). In the garden of Gethsemane the three best of them slept when they should have watched and prayed. In the hour of His betrayal they all forsook Him and fled, and worst of all, Peter, the most forward of the twelve, denied his Master three times with an oath.

Even after the resurrection, you see the same unbelief and hardness of heart cling to them; though they saw their Lord with their eyes, and touched Him with their hands, even then some doubted. So weak were they in faith! So slow of heart were they to "believe all that the prophets had spoken" (Luke 24:25). So backward were they in understanding the meaning of our Lord's words, and actions, and life, and death.

But what do you see in our Lord's behavior towards these disciples all through His ministry? You see nothing but unchanging pity, compassion, kindness, gentleness, patience, long-suffering, and love. He does not cast them off for their stupidity. He does not reject them for their unbelief. He does not dismiss them forever for cowardice. He teaches them as they are able to bear. He leads them on step by step, as a nurse does an infant when it first begins to walk. He sends them kind messages as soon as He is risen from the dead. "Go," He said to the women, "Go tell my brethren that they go into Galilee, and there they shall see me" (Matt. 28:10). He gathers them round Himself once more. He restores Peter to his place, and bids him "feed my sheep" (John 21:17). He condescends to sojourn with them forty days before He finally ascends. He commissions them to go forth as His messengers, and preach the Gospel to the Gentiles. He blesses them in parting, and encourages them with that gracious promise, "I am with you always, even unto the end of the world" (Matt. 28:20). Truly this was a love that passes knowledge. This is not the manner of man.

Let all the world know that the Lord Christ is full of pity, and of tender mercy. He will not break the bruised reed, nor quench the smoking flax. As a father pities his children, so He pities them that fear Him. As one whom his mother comforts, so will He comfort His people (James 5:11; Matt. 12:20; Ps. 103:13; Isa. 66:13). He cares for the lambs of His flock as well as for the old sheep. He cares for the sick and feeble ones of His fold as well as for the strong. It is written that He will carry them in His bosom, rather than let one of them be lost (Isa. 40:11). He cares for the least members of His body, as well as for the greatest. He cares for the babes of His family as well as the grown-up men. He cares for the tenderest little plants in His garden as well as for the cedar of Lebanon. All are in His book of life, and all are under His charge. All are given to Him in an everlasting covenant, and He has undertaken, in spite of all weaknesses, to bring every one safe home. Only let a sinner lay hold on Christ by faith and then, however feeble, Christ's word is pledged to him, "I will never leave thee nor forsake thee." He may correct him occasionally in love. He may gently reprove him at times. But He will never, never give him up. The devil shall never pluck him from Christ's hand.

Let all the world know that the Lord Jesus will not cast away His believing people because of shortcomings and infirmities. The husband does not put away his wife because he finds failings in her. The mother does not forsake her infant because it is weak, feeble, and ignorant. And the Lord Christ does not cast off poor sinners who have committed their souls into His hands because He sees in them blemishes and imperfections. Oh, no! It is His glory to pass over the faults of His people, and heal their backslidings—to make much of their weak graces and to pardon their many faults. The eleventh of Hebrews is a wonderful chapter. It is marvelous to observe how the Holy Ghost speaks of the worthies whose names are recorded in that chapter. The faith of the Lord's people is there brought forward and had in remembrance. But the faults of many a one, which might easily have been brought up also, are left alone, and not mentioned at all.

Who is there now among the readers of this chapter who desires after salvation, but is afraid to become decided, lest by-and-by he should fall away? Consider, I beseech you, the tenderness and patience of the Lord Jesus and be afraid no more. Fear not to take up the cross and come out boldly from the world. That same Lord and Savior who bore with the disciples is ready and willing to bear with you. If you stumble, He will raise you. If you err, He will gently bring you back. If you faint, He will revive you. He will not lead you out of Egypt, and then suffer you to perish in the wilderness. He will conduct you safely into the Promised Land. Only commit yourself to His guidance, and then, my soul for yours, He shall carry you safely home. Only hear Christ's voice, and follow Him, and you shall never perish.

Who is there among the readers of this chapter who has been converted and desires to do his Lord's will? Take example, this day, by your Master's gentleness and long-suffering, and learn to be tender-hearted and kind to others. Deal gently with *young beginners*. Do not expect them to know everything and understand everything all at once. Take them by the hand. Lead them on and encourage them. Believe all things, and hope all things, rather than make that heart sad which God would not have made sad. Deal gently with *backsliders*. Do not turn your back on them as if their case was hopeless. Use every lawful means to restore them to their former place. Consider yourself, and your frequent infirmities, and do as you would be done by. Alas, there is a painful absence of the Master's mind among many of His disciples. There are few churches, I fear, in the present day, which would have received Peter into communion again for many a long year, after denying his Lord. There are few believers ready to do the work of Barnabas—willing to take young converts by the hand, and encourage them at their first beginnings. Verily we want an outpouring of the Spirit upon believers almost as much as upon the world.

And now, I have only to ask my readers to make a practical use of the lessons I have brought before them. You have heard this day five things.

First. That Christ's service will not secure you against troubles. The holiest saints are liable to them.

Second. That Christ is very Man as well as God.

Third. That believers may have much weakness and infirmity, and yet be true believers.

Fourth. That Christ has all power: and

Fifth. That Christ is full of patience and kindness towards His people. Remember these five lessons, and you will do well.

Bear with me a few moments while I say a few words to impress the things you have been reading more deeply on your heart.

(1) This chapter will very likely be read by *some who know nothing of Christ's service by experience, or of Christ Himself.*

There are only too many who take no interest whatever in the things about which I have been writing. Their treasure is all below. They are wholly taken up with the things of the world.

They care nothing about the believer's conflict, and struggles, and infirmities, and doubts, and fears.

They care little whether Christ did miracles or not. It is all a matter of words, and names, and forms, about which they do not trouble themselves. They are without God in the world.

If perchance you are such a man as this, I can only warn you solemnly that your present course cannot last. You will not live forever. There must be an end. Grey hairs, age, sickness, infirmities, death—all, all are before you, and must be met one day. What will you do when that day comes?

Remember my words this day. You will find no comfort when sick and dying, unless Jesus Christ is your friend. You will discover, to your sorrow and confusion, that however much men may talk and boast, they cannot do without Christ when they come to their deathbed. You may send for ministers, and get them to read prayers, and give you the sacrament. You may go through every form and ceremony of Christianity. But if you persist in living a careless and worldly life, and despising Christ in the morning of your days, you must not be surprised if Christ leaves you to yourself in your latter end. Alas! these are solemn words, and are often sadly fulfilled: "I will laugh at your calamity; I will mock when your fear cometh" (Prov. 1:26).

Come then, this day, and be advised by one who loves your soul. Cease to do evil. Learn to do well. Forsake the foolish, and go in the path of understanding. Cast away that pride that hangs about your heart, and seek the Lord Jesus while He may be found.

Cast away that spiritual sloth that is damaging your soul, and resolve to take trouble about your Bible, your prayers, and your Sundays. Break off from a world that can never really satisfy you, and seek that treasure that alone is truly incorruptible. Oh, that the Lord's own words might find a place in your conscience! "How long, ye simple ones, will ye love simplicity? and the scorners delight in their scorning, and fools hate knowledge? Turn you at my reproof: behold I will pour out my Spirit unto you, I will make known my words unto you" (Prov. 1:22, 23). I believe the crowning sin of Judas Iscariot was that he would not seek pardon and turn again to his Lord. Beware, lest that be your sin also.

(2) This chapter will probably fall into the hands of *some who love the Lord Jesus, and believe in Him*, and yet desire to love Him better.

If you are such a man, suffer the word of exhortation and apply it to your heart.

For one thing, keep before your mind, as an ever-present truth, that *the Lord Jesus is an actual, living Person*, and deal with Him as such.

I fear the personality of our Lord is sadly lost sight of by many professors in the present day. Their talk is more about salvation than about the Savior—more about redemption than about the Redeemer—more about justification than about Jesus—more about Christ's work than about Christ's person. This is a great fault, and one that fully accounts for the dry and sapless character of the religion of many professors.

As ever, if you would grow in grace and have joy and peace in believing, beware of falling into this error. Cease to regard the Gospel as a mere collection of dry doctrines. Look at it rather as the revelation of a mighty, living Being in whose sight you are daily to live. Cease to regard it as a mere set of abstract propositions and abstruse principles and rules. Look at it as the introduction to a glorious, personal *Friend*. This is the kind of Gospel that the Apostles preached. They did not go about the world telling men of love, and mercy, and pardon, in the abstract. The leading subject of all their sermons was the loving heart of *an actual living Christ*. This is the kind of Gospel that is most calculated to promote sanctification and meetness for glory. Nothing, surely, is so likely to prepare us for that heaven where Christ's personal presence will be all, and that glory where we shall meet Christ face to face, as to realize communion with Christ, as an actual living Person here on earth. There is all the difference in the world between an idea and a person.

For another thing, try to keep before your mind, as an ever-present truth, that *the Lord Jesus is utterly unchanged.*

That Savior, in whom you trust, is the same yesterday, today, and forever. He knows no variableness, nor shadow of turning. Though high in heaven at God's right hand, He is just the same in heart that He was 2,000 years ago on earth. Remember this and you will do well.

Follow Him all through His journeys to and fro in Palestine. Mark how He received all who came to Him and cast out none. Mark how He had an ear to listen to every tale of sorrow, a hand to help every case of distress, a heart to feel for all who needed sympathy. And then say to yourself, "This same Jesus is He who is my Lord and Savior. Place and time have made no difference in Him. What He was, He is, and will be for evermore."

Surely this thought will give life and reality to your daily religion. Surely this thought will give substance and shape to your expectation of good things to come. Surely it is matter for joyful reflection, that He who was thirty-three years upon earth, and whose life we read in the Gospels, is the very Savior in whose presence we shall spend eternity.

The last word of this chapter shall be the same as the first. I want men to read the four Gospels more than they do. I want men to become better acquainted with Christ. I want unconverted men to know Jesus, that they may have eternal life through Him. I want believers to know Jesus better, that they may become more happy, more holy, and more meet for the inheritance of the saints in light. He will be the holiest man who learns to say with St. Paul, "To me to live is Christ" (Phil. 1:21).

1. Number 12 in the complete book.

"LOVEST THOU ME?"

∾

THE QUESTION THAT HEADS this chapter was addressed by Christ to the Apostle Peter. A more important question could not be asked. Two thousand years have passed away since the words were spoken. But to this very day the inquiry is most searching and useful.

A disposition to love somebody is one of the commonest feelings that God has implanted in human nature. Too often, unhappily, people set their affection on unworthy objects. I want this day to claim a place for Him who alone is worthy of all our hearts' best feelings. I want men to give some of their love to that Divine Person who loved us, and gave Himself for us. In all their loving, I would have them not forget TO LOVE CHRIST.

Allow me to press this mighty subject upon the attention of every reader of this chapter. This is no matter for mere enthusiasts and fanatics. It deserves the consideration of every reasonable Christian who believes the Bible. Our very salvation is bound up with it. Life or death, heaven or hell, depend on our ability to answer the simple question "Do you love Christ?"

There are two points that I wish to bring forward in opening up this subject.

I. In the first place, let me show *the peculiar feeling of a true Christian towards Christ*—he loves Him.

A true Christian is not a mere baptized man or woman. He is something more. He is not a person who only goes, as a matter of form, to a church or chapel on Sundays and lives all the rest of the week as if there was no God. Formality is not Christianity. Ignorant lip-worship is not true religion. The Scripture speaks expressly: "They are not all Israel which are of Israel" (Rom. 9:6). The practical lesson of those words is clear and plain. All are not true Christians who are members of the visible Church of Christ.

The true Christian is one whose religion is in his heart and life. It is felt by himself in his heart. It is seen by others in his conduct and life. He feels his sinfulness, guilt, and badness, and repents. He sees Jesus Christ to be that Divine Savior whom his soul needs, and commits himself to Him. He puts off the old man with his corrupt and carnal habits and puts on the new man. He lives a new and holy life, fighting habitually against the world, the flesh, and the devil. Christ Himself is the cornerstone of his Christianity. Ask him in what he trusts for the forgiveness of his many sins, and he will tell you in the death of Christ. Ask him in what righteousness he hopes to stand innocent at the judgment day, and he will tell you it is the righteousness of Christ. Ask him by what pattern he tries to frame his life, and he will tell you that it is the example of Christ.

But, besides all this, there is one thing in a true Christian that is eminently peculiar to him. That thing is *love* to Christ. Knowledge, faith, hope, reverence, obedience, are all marked features in a true Christian's character. But his picture would be very imperfect if you omitted his "love" to his Divine Master. He not only knows, trusts, and obeys. He goes further than this—he loves.

This peculiar mark of a true Christian is one that we find mentioned several times in the Bible. "Faith toward our Lord Jesus Christ" is an expression that many Christians are familiar with. Let it never be forgotten that love is mentioned by the Holy Ghost in almost as strong terms as faith. Great as the danger is of him "that believeth not," the danger of him that "loveth not" is equally great. Not believing and not loving are both steps to everlasting ruin.

Hear what St. Paul says to the Corinthians: "If any man love not the Lord Jesus Christ, let him be Anathema Maranatha" (1 Cor. 16:22). St. Paul allows no way of escape to the man who does not love Christ. He leaves him no loophole or excuse. A man may lack clear head-knowledge and yet be saved. He may fail in courage and be overcome by the fear of man, like Peter. He may fall tremendously, like David, and yet rise again. But if a man does not love Christ he is not in the way of life. The curse is yet upon him. He is on the broad road that leads to destruction.

Hear what St. Paul says to the Ephesians, "Grace be with all them that love our Lord Jesus Christ in sincerity" (Eph. 6:24). The Apostle is here sending his good wishes, and declaring his good will to all true Christians. Many of them, no doubt, he had never seen. Many of them in the early churches, we may be very sure, were weak in faith, and knowledge, and self-denial. How, then, shall he describe them in sending his message? What words can he use that will not discourage the weaker brethren? He chooses a sweeping expression, which exactly describes all true Christians under one common name. All had not attained to the same degree, whether in doctrine or practice. But all loved Christ in sincerity.

Hear what our Lord Jesus Christ Himself says to the Jews, "If God were your Father, ye would love me" (John 8:42). He saw His misguided enemies satisfied with their spiritual condition, on the one single ground that they were children of Abraham. He saw them, like many ignorant Christians of our own day, claiming to be God's children for no better reasons than this: that they were circumcised and belonged to the Jewish Church. He lays down the broad principle that no man is a child of God who does not love God's only begotten Son. No man has a right to call God "Father" who does not love Christ. Well would it be for many Christians if they were to remember that this mighty principle applies to them as well as to the Jews. No love to Christ—then no sonship to God.

Hear once more what our Lord Jesus Christ said to the Apostle Peter after He rose from the dead. Three times He asked him the

question, "Simon, son of Jonas, lovest thou me?" (John 21:15–17).
The occasion was remarkable. He meant gently to remind His
erring disciple of his thrice-repeated fall. He desired to call forth
from him a new confession of faith before publicly restoring to
him his commission to feed the Church. And what was the question that He asked him? He might have said:—"Believest thou?
Art thou converted? Are thou ready to confess Me? Wilt thou
obey Me?" He uses none of these expressions. He simply says,
"lovest thou me?" This is the point, He would have us know, on
which a man's Christianity hinges. Simple as the question sounded, it was most searching. Plain and easy to be understood by the
most unlearned poor man, it contains matter that tests the reality of the most advanced apostle. If a man truly loves Christ, all is
right—if not, all is wrong.

Would you know the secret of this peculiar feeling towards
Christ, which distinguishes the true Christian? You have it in the
words of St. John, "We love him because he first loved us" (1 John
4:19). That text, no doubt, applies specially to God the Father.
But it is no less true of God the Son.

A true Christian loves Christ for all He *has done* for him. He
has suffered in his stead, and died for him on the cross. He has
redeemed him from the guilt, the power, and the consequences of
sin, by His blood. He has called him by His Spirit to self-knowledge, repentance, faith, hope, and holiness. He has forgiven all his
many sins and blotted them out. He has freed him from the captivity of the world, the flesh, and the devil. He has taken him

from the brink of hell, placed him in the narrow way, and set his face toward heaven. He has given him light instead of darkness, peace of conscience instead of uneasiness, hope instead of uncertainty, life instead of death. Can you wonder that the true Christian loves Christ?

And he loves Him besides, for all that He is *still doing*. He feels that He is daily washing away his many shortcomings and infirmities, and pleading his soul's cause before God. He is daily supplying all the needs of his soul, and providing him with an hourly provision of mercy and grace. He is daily leading him by His Spirit to a city of habitation, bearing with him when he is weak and ignorant, raising him up when he stumbles and falls, protecting him against his many enemies, preparing an eternal home for him in heaven. Can you wonder that the true Christian loves Christ?

Does the debtor in jail love the friend who unexpectedly and undeservedly pays all his debts, supplies him with fresh capital, and takes him into partnership with himself? Does the prisoner in war love the man who at the risk of his own life breaks through the enemy's lines, rescues him, and sets him free? Does the drowning sailor love the man who plunges into the sea, dives after him, catches him by the hair of his head, and by a mighty effort saves him from a watery grave? A very child can answer such questions as these. Just in the same way, and upon the same principles, a true Christian loves Jesus Christ.

(a) This love to Christ is the inseparable companion of saving faith. A faith of devils, a mere intellectual faith, a man may have without love, but not that faith that saves. Love cannot usurp the office of faith. It cannot justify. It does not join the soul to Christ. It cannot bring peace to the conscience. But where there is real justifying faith in Christ, there will always be heart-love to Christ. He who is really forgiven is the man who will really love (Luke 7:47). If a man has no love to Christ, you may be sure he has no faith.

(b) Love to Christ is the mainspring of work for Christ. There is little done for His cause on earth from sense of duty, or from knowledge of what is right and proper. The heart must be interested before the hands will move and continue moving. Excitement may galvanize the Christian's hands into a fitful and spasmodic activity. But there will be no patient continuance in well-doing, no unwearied labor in missionary work at home or abroad, without love. The nurse in a hospital may do her duty properly and well, may give the sick man his medicine at the right time, may feed him, minister to him, and attend to all his wants. But there is a vast difference between that nurse and a wife tending the sickbed of a beloved husband, or a mother watching over a dying child. The one acts from a sense of duty—the other from affection and love. The one does her duty because she is paid for it—the other is what she is because of her heart. It is just the same in the matter of the service of Christ. The great workers of the Church—the men who have led forlorn hopes in the mission-field and turned the world upside down, have all been eminently lovers of Christ.

Examine the characters of Owen and Baxter, of Rutherford and George Herbert, of Leighton and Hervey, of Whitefield and Wesley, of Henry Martyn and Judson, of Bickersteth and Simeon, of Hewitson and McCheyne, of Stowell and McNeile. These men have left a mark on the world. And what was the common feature of their characters? They all loved Christ. They not only held a creed. They loved a Person, even the Lord Jesus Christ.

(c) Love to Christ is the point that we ought specially to dwell upon in teaching religion to children. Election, imputed righteousness, original sin, justification, sanctification, and even faith itself, are matters that sometimes puzzle a child of tender years. But love to Jesus seems far more within reach of their understanding. That He loved them even to His death, and that they ought to love Him in return, is a creed that meets the span of their minds. How true it is that "out of the mouths of babes and sucklings thou hast perfected praise" (Matt. 21:16)! There are myriads of Christians who know every article of the Athanasian, Nicene, and Apostolic Creeds, and yet know less of real Christianity than a little child who only knows that he loves Christ.

(d) Love to Christ is the common meeting-point of believers of every branch of Christ's Church on earth. Whether Episcopalian or Presbyterian, Baptist or Independent, Calvinist or Arminian, Methodist or Moravian, Lutheran or Reformed, Established or Free—here, at least, they are agreed. About forms and ceremonies, about Church government and modes of worship, they often differ widely. But on one point, at any rate, they are united. They have all one common feeling towards Him on whom they build their hope of salvation. They "love the Lord Jesus Christ in sincerity" (Ephes. 6:24). Many of them, perhaps, are ignorant of systematic divinity and could argue but feebly in defense of their creed. But they all know what they feel toward Him who died for their sins.—"I cannot speak much for Christ, sir," said an old, uneducated Christian woman to Dr. Chalmers; "but if I cannot speak for Him, I could die for Him!"

(e) Love to Christ will be the distinguishing mark of all saved souls in heaven. The multitude that no man can number will all be of one mind. Old differences will be merged in one common feeling. Old doctrinal peculiarities, fiercely wrangled for upon earth, will be covered over by one common sense of debt to Christ. Luther and Zwingli will no longer dispute. Wesley and Toplady will no longer waste time in controversy. Churchmen and Dissenters will no longer bite and devour one another. All will find themselves joining with one heart and voice in that hymn of praise, "Unto him that loved us, and washed us from our sin in his own blood, and hath made us kings and priests unto God and his Father; to him be glory and dominion for ever and ever. Amen" (Rev. 1:5–6).

The words that John Bunyan puts in the mouth of Mr. Standfast as he stood in the river of death are very beautiful. He said, "This river has been a terror to many; yea, the thoughts of it also have often frightened me. But now methinks I stand easy: my foot is fixed upon that on which the priests that bear the ark stood while

Israel went over Jordan. The waters indeed are to the palate bitter, and to the stomach cold; yet the thoughts of what I am going to, and of the convoy that waits for me on the other side, lie as a glowing coal at my heart. I see myself now at the end of my journey; my toilsome days are ended. I am going to see that Head which was crowned with thorns, and that Face which was spit upon for me. I have formerly lived by hearing and faith, but now I go where I shall live by sight, and be with Him in whose company I delight myself. I have loved to hear my Lord spoken of; and wherever I have seen the print of His shoe in the earth, there I have coveted to set my foot too. His name has been to me a civet-box; yea, sweeter than all perfumes! His voice to me has been most sweet; and His countenance I have more desired than they that have desired the light of the sun!" Happy are they that know something of this experience! He who would be in tune for heaven must know something of love to Christ. He who dies ignorant of that love had better never have been born.

II. Let me show, in the second place, *the peculiar marks by which love to Christ makes itself known.*

The point is one of vast importance. If there is no salvation without love to Christ—if he who does not love Christ is in peril of eternal condemnation, it becomes us all to find out very distinctly what we know about this matter. Christ is in heaven, and we are upon earth. In what way shall the man be discerned that loves Him?

Happily the point is one that it is not very hard to settle.

How do we know whether we love any person here upon earth? In what way and manner does love show itself between people in this world—between husband and wife—between parent and child—between brother and sister—between friend and friend? Let these questions be answered by common sense and observations, and I ask no more. Let these questions be honestly answered, and the knot before us is untied. How does affection show itself among ourselves?

(a) If we love a person, *we like to think about him.* We do not need to be reminded of him. We do not forget his name, or his appearance, or his character, or his opinions, or his tastes, or his position, or his occupation. He comes up before our mind's eye many a time in the day. Though perhaps far distant, he is often present in our thoughts. Well, it is just so between the true Christian and Christ! Christ "dwells in his heart," and is thought of more or less every day (Ephes. 3:17). The true Christian does not need to be reminded that he has a crucified Master. He often thinks of Him. He never forgets that He has a day, a cause, and a people, and that of His people he is one. Affection is the real secret of a good memory in religion. No worldly man can think much about Christ, unless Christ is pressed upon his notice, because he has no affection for Him. The true Christian has thoughts about Christ every day that he lives, for this one simple reason, that he loves Him.

(b) If we love a person, *we like to hear about him.* We find a pleasure in listening to those who speak of him. We feel an interest in any report that others make of him. We are all attention when others talk about him and describe his ways, his sayings, his doings, and his plans. Some may hear him mentioned with utter indifference, but our own hearts bound within us at the very sound of his name. Well, it is just so between the true Christian and Christ! The true Christian delights to hear something about his Master. He likes those sermons best that are full of Christ. He enjoys that society most in which people talk of the things which are Christ's. I have read of an old Welsh believer who used to walk several miles every Sunday to hear an English clergyman preach, though she did not understand a word of English. She was asked why she did so. She replied that this clergyman named the name of Christ so often in his sermons that it did her good. She loved even the name of her Savior.

(c) If we love a person, *we like to read about him.* What intense pleasure a letter from an absent husband gives to a wife, or a letter from an absent son to his mother. Others may see little worth notice in the letter. They can scarcely take the trouble to read it through. But those who love the writer see something in the letter that no one else can. They carry it about with them as a treasure. They read it over and over again. Well, it is just so between the true Christian and Christ! The true Christian delights to read the Scriptures, because they tell him about his beloved Savior. It is no wearisome task with him to read them. He rarely needs reminding to take his Bible with him when he goes on a journey. He cannot be happy without it. And why is all this? It is because the Scriptures testify of Him whom his soul loves, even Christ.

(d) If we love a person, *we like to please him.* We are glad to consult his tastes and opinions, to act upon his advice, and do the things that he approves. We even deny ourselves to meet his wishes, abstain from things that we know he dislikes, and learn things to do to which we are not naturally inclined, because we think it will give him pleasure. Well, it is just so between the true Christian and Christ! The true Christian studies to please Him, by being holy both in body and spirit. Show him anything in his daily practice that Christ hates, and he will give it up. Show him anything that Christ delights in, and he will follow after it. He does not murmur at Christ's requirements as being too strict and severe, as the children of the world do. To him Christ's commandments are not grievous and Christ's burden is light. And why is all this? Simply because he loves Him.

(e) If we love a person, *we like his friends.* We are favorably inclined to them, even before we know them. We are drawn to them by the common tie of common love to one and the same person. When we meet them we do not feel that we are altogether strangers. There is a bond of union between us. They love the person that we love, and that alone is an introduction. Well, it is just so between the true Christian and Christ! The true Christian regards all Christ's friends as his friends, members of the same body, children of the same family, soldiers in the same army, travelers to the same home. When he meets them, he feels as if he had long known them. He is more at home with them in a few minutes than he is with many worldly people after an acquaintance of several years. And what is the secret of all this? It is simply affection to the same Savior, and love to the same Lord.

(f) If we love a person, *we are jealous about his name and honor.* We do not like to hear him spoken against without speaking up for him and defending him. We feel bound to maintain his interests and his reputation. We regard the person who treats him ill with almost as much disfavor as if he had ill-treated us. Well, it is just so between the true Christian and Christ. The true Christian regards with a godly jealousy all efforts to disparage his Master's word, or name, or Church, or day. He will confess Him before princes, if need be, and be sensitive of the least dishonor put upon Him. He will not hold his peace and suffer his Master's cause to be put to shame without testifying against it. And why is all this? Simply because he loves Him.

(g) If we love a person, *we like to talk to him.* We tell him all our thoughts, and pour out all our heart to him. We find no difficulty in discovering subjects of conversation. However silent and reserved we may be to others, we find it easy to talk to a much-loved friend. However often we may meet, we are never at a loss for matter to talk about. We have always much to say, much to ask about, much to describe, much to communicate. Well, it is just so between the true Christian and Christ! The true Christian finds no difficulty in speaking to his Savior. Every day he has something to tell Him, and he is not happy unless he tells it. He speaks to Him in prayer every morning and night. He tells Him his wants and desires, his feelings and his fears. He asks counsel of Him in difficulty. He asks comfort of Him in trouble. He cannot help it. He must converse with his Savior continually, or he would faint by the way. And why is this? Simply because he loves Him.

(h) Finally, if we love a person, *we like to be always with him.* Thinking, and hearing, and reading, and occasionally talking are all well in their way. But when we really love people we want something more. We long to be always in their company. We wish to be continually in their society, and to hold communion with them without interruption or farewell. Well, it is just so between the true Christian and Christ. The heart of a true Christian longs for that blessed day when he will see his Master face to face, and go out no more. He longs to have done with sinning and repenting, and believing, and to begin that endless life when he shall see as he has been seen, and sin no more. He has found it sweet to live by faith, and he feels it will be sweeter still to live by sight. He has found it pleasant to hear of Christ, and talk of Christ, and read of Christ. How much more pleasant will it be to see Christ with his own eyes, and never to leave Him any more! "Better," he feels, "is the sight of the eyes than the wandering of the desires" (Eccles. 6:9). And why is all this? Simply because he loves Him.

Such are the marks by which true love may be discovered. They are all plain, simple, and easy to be understood. There is nothing dark, abstruse, and mysterious about them. Use them honestly, and handle them fairly, and you cannot fail to get some light on the subject of this chapter.

Perhaps you had a beloved son in the army at the time of a great war. Perhaps he was actively engaged in that war, and in the very midst of the struggle. Cannot you remember how strong, and deep, and anxious your feelings were about that son?—That was love!

Perhaps you have known what it is to have a beloved husband in the navy, often called from home by duty, often separated from you for many months and even years. Cannot you recollect your sorrowful feelings at that time of separation?—That was love!

Perhaps you have at this moment a beloved brother in London, launched for the first time amidst the temptations of a great city, in order to make his way in business. How will he turn out? How will he get on? Will you ever see him again? Do you not know that you often think about that brother?—That is affection!

Perhaps you are engaged to be married to a person every way suited to you. But prudence makes it necessary to defer the marriage to a distant period, and duty makes it necessary to be at a distance from the one you have promised to make your wife. Must you not confess that she is often in your thoughts?—Must you not confess that you like to hear of her, and hear from her, and that you long to see her?—That is affection!

I speak of things that are familiar to everyone. I need not

dwell upon them any further. They are as old as the hills. They are understood all over the world. There is hardly a branch of Adam's family that does not know something of affection and love. Then let it never be said that we cannot find out whether a Christian really loves Christ. It can be known; it may be discovered; the proofs are all ready to your hand. You have heard them this very day. Love to the Lord Jesus Christ is no hidden, secret, impalpable thing. It is like the light—it will be seen. It is like sound—it will be heard. It is like heat—it will be felt. Where it exists it cannot be hid. Where it cannot be seen you may be sure there is none.

It is time for me to draw this chapter to a conclusion. But I cannot end without an effort to press its subject home to the individual conscience of each into whose hands it has fallen. I do it in all love and affection. My heart's desire and prayer to God, in writing this book, is to do good to souls.

(1) Let me ask you, for one thing, to look the question in the face, which Christ asked of Peter, and *try to answer it* for yourself. Look at it seriously. Examine it carefully. Weigh it well. After reading all that I have said about it, can you honestly say that you love Christ?

It is no answer to tell me that you believe the truth of Christianity, and hold the articles of the Christian faith. Such religion as this will never save your soul. The devils believe in a certain way, and tremble (James 2:19). True, saving Christianity is not the mere believing a certain set of opinions, and holding a certain set of notions. Its essence is knowing, trusting, and loving a certain living Person who died for us—even Christ the Lord. The early Christians, like Phoebe, and Persis, and Tryphena, and Tryphosa, and Gaius, and Philemon, knew little, probably, of dogmatic theology. But they all had this grand leading feature in their religion, they loved Christ.

It is no answer to tell me that you disapprove of a religion of feelings. If you mean by that that you dislike a religion consisting of nothing but feelings, I agree with you entirely. But if you mean to shut out feelings altogether, you can know little of Christianity. The Bible teaches us plainly that a man may have good feelings without any true religion. But it teaches us no less plainly that there can be no true religion without some feeling towards Christ.

It is vain to conceal that if you do not love Christ, your soul is in great danger. You can have no saving faith now while you live. You are unfit for heaven when you die. He who lives without love to Christ can be sensible of no obligation to Him. He who dies without love to Christ could never be happy in that heaven where Christ is all, and in all. Awake to know the peril of your position. Open your eyes. Consider your ways, and be wise. I can only warn you as a friend. But I do it with all my heart and soul. May God grant that this warning may not be in vain!

(2) In the next place, if you do not love Christ, let me tell you plainly what is *the reason*. You have no sense of debt to Him. You have no feeling of obligation to Him. You have no abiding recol-

lection of having got anything from Him. This being the case it is not likely, it is not probable, it is not reasonable that you should love Him.

There is but one remedy for this state of things. That remedy is self-knowledge, and the teaching of the Holy Ghost. The eyes of your understanding must be opened. You must find out what you are by nature. You must discover that grand secret, your guilt and emptiness in God's sight.

Perhaps you never read your Bible at all, or only read an occasional chapter as a mere matter of form, without interest, understanding, or self-application. Take my advice this day, and change your plan. Begin to read the Bible like a man in earnest, and never rest till you become familiar with it. Read what the law of God requires, as expounded by the Lord Jesus in the fifth of St. Matthew. Read how St. Paul describes human nature in the first two chapters of his Epistle to the Romans. Study such passages as these with prayer for the Spirit's teaching, and then say whether you are not a debtor to God and a debtor in mighty need of a Friend like Christ.

Perhaps you are one who has never known anything of real, hearty, business-like prayer. You have been used to regard religion as an affair of churches, chapels, forms, services, and Sundays, but not as a thing requiring the serious, heartfelt attention of the inward man. Take my advice this day and change your plan. Begin the habit of real, earnest pleading with God about your soul. Ask Him for light, teaching, and self-knowledge.

Beseech Him to show you anything you need to know for the saving of your soul. Do this with all your heart and mind, and I have no doubt that before long you will feel your need of Christ.

The advice I offer may seem simple and old-fashioned. Do not despise it on that account. It is the good old way in which millions have walked already and found peace to their souls. Not to love Christ is to be in imminent danger of eternal ruin. To see your need of Christ and your amazing debt to Christ is the first step towards loving Him. To know yourself and find out your real condition before God is the only way to see your need. To search God's Book and ask God for light in prayer is the right course by which to attain saving knowledge. Do not be above taking the advice I offer. Take it and be saved.

(3) In the last place, if you really know anything of love towards Christ, accept two parting words of *comfort and counsel.* The Lord grant they may do you good.

For one thing, if you love Christ in deed and truth, rejoice in the thought that you have good evidence about the state of your soul. Love, I tell you this day, is an evidence of grace.

What though you are sometimes perplexed with doubts and fears? What though you find it hard to say whether your faith is genuine and your grace real? What though your eyes are often so dimmed with tears that you cannot clearly see your calling and election of God? Still there is ground for hope and strong consolation if your heart can testify that you love Christ. Where there is true love, there is faith and grace. You would not love Him if

He had not done something for you. Your very love is a token for good.

For another thing, if you love Christ, never be ashamed to let others see it and know it. Speak for Him. Witness for Him. Live for Him. Work for Him. If He has loved you and washed you from your sins in His own blood, you never need shrink from letting others know that you feel it, and love Him in return.

"Man," said a thoughtless, ungodly English traveler to a North American Indian convert, "Man, what is the reason that you make so much of Christ, and talk so much about Him? What has this Christ done for you, that you should make so much ado about Him?"

The converted Indian did not answer him in words. He gathered together some dry leaves and moss and made a ring with them on the ground. He picked up a live worm and put it in the middle of the ring. He struck a light and set the moss and leaves on fire. The flame soon rose and the heat scorched the worm. It writhed in agony, and after trying in vain to escape on every side, curled itself up in the middle, as if about to die in despair. At that moment the Indian reached forth his hand, took up the worm gently and placed it on his bosom. "Stranger," he said to the Englishman, "Do you see that worm? I was that perishing creature. I was dying in my sins, hopeless, helpless, and on the brink of eternal fire. It was Jesus Christ who put forth the arm of His power. It was Jesus Christ who delivered me with the hand of His grace, and plucked me from everlasting burnings. It was Jesus

Christ who placed me, a poor sinful worm, near the heart of His love. Stranger, that is the reason why I talk of Jesus Christ and make much of Him. I am not ashamed of it, because I love Him."

If we know anything of love to Christ, may we have the mind of this North American Indian! May we never think that we can love Christ too well, live to Him too thoroughly, confess Him too boldly, lay ourselves out for Him too heartily! Of all the things that will surprise us in the resurrection morning, this, I believe, will surprise us most: that we did not love Christ more before we died.

1. Number 15 in the complete book.

"CHRIST IS ALL"

∾

"CHRIST IS ALL." *(Colossians 3:11)*

THE WORDS OF THE TEXT that heads this page are few, short, and soon spoken; but they contain great things. Like those golden sayings, "To me to live is Christ"—"I live, yet not I, but Christ liveth in me"—they are singularly rich and suggestive (Phil. 1:21; Gal. 2:20).

These three words are the essence and substance of Christianity. If our hearts can really go along with them, it is well with our souls. If not, we may be sure we have yet much to learn.

Let me try to set before my readers in what sense "Christ is all"; and let me ask them, as they read, to judge themselves honestly, that they may not make shipwreck in the judgment of the last day.

I purposely close this volume with a chapter on this remarkable text. Christ is the mainspring both of doctrinal and practical Christianity. A right knowledge of Christ is essential to a right knowledge of sanctification as well as justification. He who follows after holiness will make no progress unless he gives to Christ His rightful place. I began the volume with a plain statement about sin. Let me end it with an equally plain statement about Christ.

I. First of all, let us understand that *Christ is all, in all the counsels of God concerning man.*

(**a**) There was a time when this earth had no being. Solid as the mountains look, boundless as the sea appears, high as the stars in heaven look—they once did not exist. And man, with all the high thoughts he now has of himself, was a creature unknown.

And where was Christ then?

Even then Christ was "with God"—and "was God"—and was "equal with God" (John 1:1; Phil. 2:6). Even then He was the beloved Son of the Father: "Thou lovedst me," He says, "before the foundation of the world."—"I had glory with thee before the world began."—"I was set up from everlasting, from the beginning, or ever the earth was" (John 17:5, 24; Prov. 8:23). Even then He was the Savior "foreordained before the foundation of the world" (1 Peter 1:20), and believers were "chosen in him" (Ephes. 1:4).

(**b**) There came a time when this earth was created in its present order. Sun, moon, and stars—sea, land, and all their inhabitants, were called into being and made out of chaos and confusion. And, last of all, man was formed out of the dust of the ground.

And where was Christ then?

Hear what the Scripture says: "All things were made by him, and without him was not any thing made that was made" (John 1:3). "By him were all things created, that are in heaven and that are in earth" (Colos. 1:16). "And thou, Lord, in the beginning hast laid the foundation of the earth; and the heavens are the works of thine hands" (Heb. 1:10). "When he prepared the heavens, I was there: when he set a compass upon the face of the depth: when he established the clouds above: when he strengthened the foundations of the deep: when he gave to the sea his decree, that the water should not pass his commandment: when he appointed the foundations of the earth: then I was by him, as one brought up with Him" (Prov. 8:27–30). Can we wonder that the Lord Jesus, in His preaching, should continually draw lessons from the book of nature? When He spoke of the sheep, the fish, the ravens, the corn, the lilies, the fig-tree, the vine—He spoke of things which He Himself had made.

(c) There came a day when sin entered the world.—Adam and Eve ate the forbidden fruit, and fell. They lost that holy nature in which they were first formed. They forfeited the friendship and favor of God and became guilty, corrupt, helpless, hopeless sinners. Sin came as a barrier between themselves and their holy Father in heaven. Had He dealt with them according to their deserts, there had been nothing before them but death, hell, and everlasting ruin.

And where was Christ then?

In that very day He was revealed to our trembling parents, as the only hope of salvation. The very day they fell, they were told that "the seed of the woman should yet bruise the serpent's head"—that a Savior born of a woman should overcome the devil and win for sinful man an entrance to eternal life (Gen. 3:15). Christ was held up as the true light of the world, in the very day of the Fall; and never has any name been made known from that day by which souls could be saved, excepting His. By Him all saved souls have entered heaven, from Adam downwards; and without Him none have ever escaped hell.

(d) There came a time when the world seemed sunk and buried in ignorance of God. After 4,000 years the nations of the earth appeared to have clean forgotten the God that made them. Egyptian, Assyrian, Persian, Grecian, and Roman empires had done nothing but spread superstition and idolatry. Poets, historians, philosophers had proved that, with all their intellectual powers, they had no right knowledge of God; and that man, left to himself, was utterly corrupt. "The world, by wisdom, knew not God" (1 Cor. 1:21). Excepting a few despised Jews in a corner of the earth, the whole world was dead in ignorance and sin.

And what did Christ do then?

He left the glory He had had from all eternity with the Father, and came down into the world to provide salvation. He took our nature upon Him, and was born as a man. As a man He did the will of God perfectly, which we all had left undone: as a man He suffered on the cross the wrath of God, which we ought to have suffered. He brought in everlasting righteousness for us. He redeemed us from the curse of a broken law. He opened a fountain for all sin and uncleanness. He died for our sins. He rose again for our justification. He ascended to God's right hand, and there sat down, waiting till His enemies should be made His footstool. And there He sits now, offering salvation to all who will come to Him, interceding for all who believe in Him, and managing by God's appointment all that concerns the salvation of souls.

(e) There is a time coming when sin shall be cast out from this world.—Wickedness shall not always flourish unpunished—Satan shall not always reign—creation shall not always groan, being burdened. There shall be a time of restitution of all things. There shall be a new heaven and a new earth, wherein dwelleth righteousness, and the earth shall be full of the knowledge of the Lord as the waters cover the sea (Rom. 8:22; Acts 3:21; 2 Pet. 3:13; Isa. 11:9).

And where shall Christ be then? And what shall He do?

Christ Himself shall be King. He shall return to this earth and make all things new. He shall come in the clouds of heaven with power and great glory, and the kingdoms of the world shall become His. The heathen shall be given to Him for His inheritance, and the uttermost parts of the earth for His possession. To Him every knee shall bow, and every tongue shall confess that He is Lord. His dominion shall be an everlasting dominion, which shall not pass away, and His kingdom that which shall not be destroyed (Matt. 24:30; Rev. 11:15; Ps. 2:8; Phil. 2:10, 11; Dan. 7:14).

(f) There is a day coming when all men shall be judged. The sea shall give up the dead which are in it, and death and hell shall deliver up the dead which are in them. All that sleep in the grave shall awake and come forth, and all shall be judged according to their works (Rev. 20:13; Dan. 12:2).

And where will Christ be then?

Christ Himself will be the Judge. "The Father hath committed all judgment unto the Son."—"When the Son of man shall come in his glory, then shall he sit upon the throne of his glory:— and before him shall be gathered all nations: and he shall separate them one from another, as a shepherd divideth the sheep from the goats."—"We must all appear before the judgment seat of Christ: that every one may receive the things done in his body, according to that he hath done, whether it be good or bad" (John 5:22; Matt. 25:32; 2 Cor. 5:10).

Now if any reader of this chapter thinks little of Christ, let him know this day that he is very unlike God! You are of one mind, and God is of another. You think it enough to give Christ a *little* honor—a *little* reverence—a *little* respect. But in all the eternal counsels of God the Father, in creation, redemption, restitution, and judgment—in all these, Christ is "all."

Surely we shall do well to consider these things. Surely it is not written in vain, "He that honoreth not the Son, honoreth not the Father which hath sent him" (John 5:23).

II. In the second place, let us understand that *"Christ is all" in the inspired books that make up the Bible.*

In every part of both Testaments, Christ is to be found—dimly and indistinctly at the beginning—more clearly and plainly in the middle—fully and completely at the end—but really and substantially everywhere.

Christ's sacrifice and death for sinners, and Christ's kingdom and future glory, are the light we must bring to bear on any book of Scripture we read. Christ's cross and Christ's crown are the clue we must hold fast if we would find our way through Scripture difficulties. Christ is the only key that will unlock many of the dark places of the Word. Some people complain that they do not understand the Bible. And the reason is very simple. They do not use the key. To them the Bible is like the hieroglyphics in Egypt. It is a mystery, just because they do not know and employ the key.

(a) It was Christ crucified who was set forth in every Old Testament sacrifice. Every animal slain and offered on an altar was a practical confession that a Savior was looked for who would die for sinners—a Savior who should take away man's sin, by suffering, as his Substitute and Sin-bearer, in his stead (1 Peter 3:18). It is absurd to suppose that an unmeaning slaughter of innocent beasts, without a distinct object in view, could please the eternal God!

(b) It was Christ to whom Abel looked when he offered a better sacrifice than Cain. Not only was the heart of Abel better than that of his brother, but he showed his knowledge of vicarious sacrifice and his faith in an atonement. He offered the firstlings of his flock, with the blood thereof, and in so doing declared his belief that without shedding of blood there is no remission (Heb. 11:4).

(c) It was Christ of whom Enoch prophesied in the days of abounding wickedness before the flood.—"Behold," he said, "the Lord cometh with ten thousands of his saints, to execute judgment upon all" (Jude 15).

(d) It was Christ to whom Abraham looked when he dwelt in tents in the land of promise. He believed that in his seed—in one born of his family—all the nations of the earth should be blessed. By faith he saw Christ's day, and was glad (John 8:56).

(e) It was Christ of whom Jacob spoke to his sons, as he lay dying. He marked out the tribe out of which He would be born, and foretold that "gathering together" unto Him, which is yet to be accomplished. "The sceptre shall not depart from Judah, nor the law-giver from between his feet, until Shiloh come, and unto him shall the gathering of the people be" (Gen. 49:10).

(f) It was Christ who was the substance of the ceremonial law, which God gave to Israel by the hand of Moses. The morning and evening sacrifice—the continual shedding of blood—the altar —the mercy-seat—the high priest—the Passover—the day of atonement—the scapegoat:—all these were so many pictures, types, and emblems of Christ and His work. God had compassion upon the weakness of His people. He taught them "Christ" line upon line, and, as we teach little children, by similitudes. It was in this sense especially that "the law was a school-master to lead" the Jews "unto Christ" (Gal. 3:24).

(g) It was Christ to whom God directed the attention of Israel by all the daily miracles that were done before their eyes in the wilderness. The pillar of cloud and fire that guided them—the manna from heaven that every morning fed them—the water from the smitten rock that followed them—all and each were figures of Christ. The brazen serpent, on that memorable occasion when the plague of fiery serpents was sent upon them, was an emblem of Christ (1 Cor. 10:4; John 3:14).

(h) It was Christ of whom figures of old were types. Joshua, and David, and Gideon, and Jephthah, and Samson, and all the rest whom God raised up to deliver Israel from captivity—all were emblems of Christ. Weak and unstable and faulty as some of them were, they were set for example of better things in the distant future. All were meant to remind the tribes of that far higher Deliverer who was yet to come.

(i) It was Christ of whom David the king was a type. Anointed and chosen when few gave him honor—despised and rejected by Saul and all the tribes of Israel—persecuted and obliged to flee for his life—a man of sorrow all his life, and yet at length a conqueror—in all these things David represented Christ.

(j) It was Christ of whom all the prophets from Isaiah to Malachi spoke. They saw through a glass darkly. They sometimes dwelt on His sufferings, and sometimes on His glory that should follow (1 Peter 1:11). They did not always mark out for us the distinction between Christ's first coming and Christ's second coming. Like two candles in a straight line, one behind the other, they sometimes saw both the advents at the same time, and spoke of them in one breath. They were sometimes moved by the Holy Ghost to write of the times of Christ crucified, and sometimes of Christ's kingdom in the latter days. But Jesus dying, or Jesus reigning, was the thought you will ever find uppermost in their minds.

(k) It is Christ, I need hardly say, of whom the whole New Testament is full. The Gospels are "Christ" living, speaking, and moving among men. The Acts are "Christ" preached, published, and proclaimed. The Epistles are "Christ" written of, explained, and exalted. But all through, from first to last, there is one name above every other, and that is the name of Christ.

I charge every reader of this chapter to ask himself frequently what the Bible is to him. Is it a Bible in which you have found nothing more than good moral precepts and sound advice? Or is it a Bible in which you have found Christ? Is it a Bible in which "Christ is all"? If not, I tell you plainly, you have hitherto used your Bible to very little purpose. You are like a man who studies the solar system and leaves out in his studies the sun, which is the center of all. It is no wonder if you find your Bible a dull book!

III. In the third place, let us understand *that "Christ is all" in the religion of all true Christians on earth.*

In saying this, I wish to guard myself against being misunderstood. I hold the absolute necessity of the election of God the

Father, and the sanctification of God the Spirit, in order to effect the salvation of everyone who is saved. I hold that there is a perfect harmony and unison in the action of the three Persons of the Trinity, in bringing any man to glory, and that all three cooperate and work a joint work in his deliverance from sin and hell. Such as the Father is, such is the Son, and such is the Holy Ghost. The Father is merciful, the Son is merciful, the Holy Ghost is merciful. The same three who said at the beginning, "Let us create," said also, "Let us redeem and save." I hold that everyone who reaches heaven will ascribe all the glory of his salvation to Father, Son, and Holy Ghost, three Persons in one God.

But, at the same time, I see clear proof in Scripture that it is the mind of the blessed Trinity that Christ should be prominently and distinctly exalted in the matter of saving souls. Christ is set forth as the "Word," through whom God's love to sinners is made known. Christ's incarnation and atoning death on the cross are the great cornerstone on which the whole plan of salvation rests. Christ is the way and door, by which alone approaches to God are to be made. Christ is the root into which all elect sinners must be grafted. Christ is the only meeting-place between God and man, between heaven and earth, between the Holy Trinity and the poor sinful child of Adam. It is Christ whom God the Father has "sealed" and appointed to convey life to a dead world (John 6:27). It is Christ to whom the Father has given a people to be brought to glory. It is Christ of whom the Spirit testifies, and to whom He always leads a soul for pardon and peace. In short, it has "pleased the Father that in Christ all fullness should dwell" (Coloss. 1:19). What the sun is in the firmament of heaven, that Christ is in true Christianity.

I say these things by way of explanation. I want my readers clearly to understand that in saying "Christ is all," I do not mean to shut out the work of the Father and of the Spirit. Now let me show what I do mean.

(a) Christ is *all in a sinner's justification before God.*

Through Him alone we can have peace with a Holy God. By Him alone we can have admission into the presence of the Most High, and stand there without fear. "We have boldness and access with confidence by the faith of him." In Him alone can God be just, and justify the ungodly (Ephes. 3:12; Rom. 3:26).

Wherewith can any mortal man come before God? What can we bring as a plea for acquittal before that Glorious Being, in whose eyes the very heavens are not clean?

Shall we say that we have done our duty to God? Shall we say that we have done our duty to our neighbor? Shall we bring forward our prayers?—our faithfulness?—our morality?—our amendments?—our churchgoing? Shall we ask to be accepted because of any of these?

Which of these things will stand the searching inspection of God's eye? Which of them will actually justify us? Which of them will carry us clear through judgment, and land us safe in glory?

None, none, none! Take any commandment of the ten, and let us examine ourselves by it. We have broken it repeatedly. We cannot answer God one of a thousand.—Take any of us, and look narrowly into our ways—and we are nothing but sinners. There is but one verdict: we are all guilty—all deserve hell—all ought to die. Wherewith can we come before God?

We must come in the name of Jesus—standing on no other ground—pleading no other plea than this, "Christ died on the cross for the ungodly, and I trust in Him. Christ died for me, and I believe on Him."

The *garment* of our Elder Brother—the righteousness of Christ—this is the only robe that can cover us and enable us to stand in the light of heaven without shame.

The *name* of Jesus is the only name by which we shall obtain an entrance through the gate of eternal glory. If we come to that gate in our own names, we are lost, we shall not be admitted, we shall knock in vain. If we come in the name of Jesus, it is a passport and Shibboleth, and we shall enter and live.

The *mark* of the blood of Christ is the only mark that can save us from destruction. When the angels are separating the children of Adam in the last day, if we are not found marked with that atoning blood, we had better never have been born.

Oh, let us never forget that Christ must be "all" to that soul who would be justified!—We must be content to go to heaven as beggars—saved by free grace, simply as believers in Jesus—or we shall never be saved at all.

Is there a thoughtless, worldly soul among the readers of this book? Is there one who thinks to reach heaven by saying hastily at the last, "Lord have mercy on me" without Christ? Friend, you are sowing misery for yourself, and unless you alter you will awake to endless woe.

Is there a proud, formal soul among the readers of this book? Is there anyone thinking to make himself fit for heaven and good enough to pass muster by his own doings?—Brother, you are building a Babel, and you will never reach heaven in your present state.

But is there a laboring, heavy-laden one among the readers of this book? Is there one who wants to be saved, and feels a vile sinner? I say to such an one, "Come to Christ, and He shall save you. Come to Christ, and cast the burden of your soul on Him. Fear not: only believe."

Do you fear wrath? Christ can deliver you from the wrath to come.—Do you feel the curse of a broken law? Christ can redeem you from the curse of the law.—Do you feel far away? Christ has suffered, to bring you nigh to God.—Do you feel unclean? Christ's blood can cleanse all sin away.—Do you feel imperfect? You shall be complete in Christ.—Do you feel as if you were nothing? Christ shall be "all in all" to your soul.—Never did saint reach heaven with any tale but this, "I was washed and made white in the blood of the Lamb" (Rev. 7:14).

(b) But again, Christ is not only all in the justification of a true Christian, but He is also *all in his sanctification.*

I would not have anyone misunderstand me. I do not mean for a moment to undervalue the work of the Spirit. But this I say, that no man is ever holy till he comes to Christ and is united to Him. Till then his works are dead works, and he has no holiness at all.—First you must be joined to Christ, and then you shall be holy. "Without Him—separate from Him—you can do nothing" (John 15:5).

And no man can grow in holiness except he abides in Christ. Christ is the great root from which every believer must draw his strength to go forward. The Spirit is His special gift, His purchased gift for His people. A believer must not only "receive Christ Jesus the Lord," but "walk in him, and be rooted and built up in him" (Col. 2:6, 7).

Would you be holy? Then Christ is the manna you must daily eat, like Israel in the wilderness of old. Would you be holy? Then Christ must be the rock from which you must daily drink the living water. Would you be holy? Then you must be ever looking unto Jesus—looking at His cross, and learning fresh motives for a closer walk with God—looking at His example, and taking Him for your pattern. Looking at Him, you would become like Him. Looking at Him, your face would shine without your knowing it. Look less at yourself and more at Christ, and you will find besetting sins dropping off and leaving you, and your eyes enlightened more and more every day (Heb. 12:2; 2 Cor. 3:18).

The true secret of coming up out of the wilderness is to come up "leaning on the Beloved" (Song of Solomon 8:5). The true way to be strong is to realize our weakness and to feel that Christ must be all. The true way to grow in grace is to make use of

Christ as a fountain for every minute's necessities. We ought to employ Him as the prophet's wife employed the oil—not only to pay our debts, but to live on also. We should strive to be able to say, "The life that I now live in the flesh I live by the faith of the Son of God, who loved me, and gave himself for me" (2 Kings 4:7; Gal. 2:20).

I pity those who try to be holy without Christ! Your labor is all in vain. You are putting money in a bag with holes. You are pouring water into a sieve. You are rolling a huge round stone uphill. You are building up a wall with untempered mortar. Believe me, you are beginning at the wrong end. You must come to Christ first, and He shall give you His sanctifying Spirit. You must learn to say with Paul, "I can do all things through Christ which strengtheneth me" (Phil. 4:13).

(c) But again, Christ is not only all in the sanctification of a true Christian, but *all in His comfort in time present.*

A saved soul has many sorrows. He has a body like other men—weak and frail. He has a heart like other men—and often a more sensitive one, too. He has trials and losses to bear like others—and often more. He has his share of bereavements, deaths, disappointments, crosses. He has the world to oppose—a place in life to fill blamelessly—unconverted relatives to bear with patiently—persecutions to endure—and a death to die.

And who is sufficient for these things? What shall enable a believer to bear all this? Nothing but "the consolation there is in Christ" (Phil. 2:1).

Jesus is indeed the brother born for adversity. He is the friend who sticks closer than a brother, and He alone can comfort His people. He can be touched with the feeling of their infirmities, for He suffered Himself (Heb. 4:15). He knows what sorrow is, for He was a Man of sorrows. He knows what an aching body is, for His body was racked with pain. He cried, "All my bones are out of joint" (Ps. 22:14). He knows what poverty and weariness are, for He was often wearied and had not where to lay His head. He knows what family unkindness is, for even His brethren did not believe Him. He had no honor in His own house.

And Jesus knows exactly how to comfort His afflicted people. He knows how to pour in oil and wine into the wounds of the spirit—how to fill up gaps in empty hearts—how to speak a word in season to the weary—how to heal the broken heart—how to make all our bed in sickness—how to draw nigh when we are faint, and say, "Fear not: I am thy salvation" (Lam. 3:57).

We talk of sympathy being pleasant. There is no sympathy like that of Christ. In all our afflictions He is afflicted. He knows our sorrows. In all our pain He is pained, and like the good Physician, He will not measure out to us one drop of sorrow too much. David once said, "In the multitude of my thoughts within me, thy comforts delight my soul" (Ps. 94:19). Many a believer, I am sure, could say as much. "If the Lord himself had not stood by me, the deep waters would have gone over my soul" (Ps. 124:5).

How a believer gets through all his troubles appears wonderful. How he is carried through the fire and water he passes through seems past comprehension. But the true account of it is just this—that Christ is not only justification and sanctification, but consolation also.

Oh, you who want unfailing comfort, I commend you to Christ! In Him alone there is no failure. Rich men are disappointed in their treasures. Learned men are disappointed in their books. Husbands are disappointed in their wives. Wives are disappointed in their husbands. Parents are disappointed in their children. Statesmen are disappointed when, after many a struggle, they attain place and power. They find out, to their cost, that it is more pain than pleasure—that it is disappointment, annoyance, incessant trouble, worry, vanity, and vexation of spirit. But no man was ever disappointed in Christ.

(d) But as Christ is all in the comforts of a true Christian in time present, so Christ *is all in his hopes for time to come.*

Few men and women, I suppose, are to be found who do not indulge in hopes of some kind about their souls. But the hopes of the vast majority are nothing but vain fancies. They are built on no solid foundation. No living man but the real child of God—the sincere, thoroughgoing Christian—can give a reasonable account of the hope that is in him. No hope is reasonable that is not Scriptural.

A true Christian has a good hope when he looks forward: the worldly man has none. A true Christian sees light in the distance: the worldly man sees nothing but darkness. And what is the hope of a true Christian? It is just this—that Jesus Christ is coming again, coming without sin—coming with all His people, coming to wipe away every tear—coming to raise His sleeping saints from the grave—coming to gather together all His family, that they may be for ever with Him.

Why is a believer patient? because he looks for the coming of the Lord. He can bear hard things without murmuring. He knows the time is short. He waits quietly for the King.

Why is he moderate in all things? Because he expects his Lord soon to return. His treasure is in heaven, his good things are yet to come. The world is not his rest, but an inn; and an inn is not home. He knows that "He that shall come will soon come, and will not tarry." Christ is coming, and that is enough (Heb. 10:37).

This is indeed a "blessed hope" (Titus 2:13)! Now is the school-time—then the eternal holiday. Now is the tossing on the waves of a troublesome world—then the quiet harbor. Now is the scattering—then the gathering. Now is the time of sowing—then the harvest. Now is the working season—then the wages. Now is the cross—then the crown.

People talk of their "expectations" and hopes from this world. None have such solid expectations as a saved soul. He can say, "My soul, wait thou only upon God; my expectation is from him" (Ps. 62:5).

In all true saving religion Christ is all: all in justification—all in comfort—all in hope. Blessed is that mother's child that *knows* it, and far more blessed is he that feels it too. Oh that men would prove themselves, and see what they know of it for their own souls!

IV. One thing more I will add, and then I have done. Let us understand that *Christ will be all in heaven.*

I cannot dwell long on this point. I have not power, if I had space and room. I can ill describe things unseen and a world unknown. But this I know, that all men and women who reach heaven will find that even there also "Christ is all."

Like the altar in Solomon's temple, Christ crucified will be the grand object in heaven. That altar struck the eye of every one who entered the temple gates. It was a great brazen altar, twenty cubits broad—as broad as the front of the temple itself (2 Chron. 3:4; 4:1). So in like manner will Jesus fill the eyes of all who enter glory. In the midst of the throne and surrounded by adoring angels and saints, there will be "the Lamb that was slain." And "the Lamb shall be the light" of the place (Rev. 5:6; 21:23).

The *praise* of the Lord Jesus will be the eternal song of all the inhabitants of heaven. They will say with a loud voice, "Worthy is the Lamb that was slain. Blessing, and honor, and glory, and power, be to him that sitteth on the throne, and to the Lamb for ever and ever" (Rev. 5:12, 13).

The *service* of the Lord Jesus will be one eternal occupation of all the inhabitants of heaven. We shall "serve him day and night in his temple" (Rev. 7:13). Blessed is the thought that we shall at length attend on Him without distraction, and work for Him without weariness.

The *presence* of Christ Himself shall be one everlasting enjoyment of the inhabitants of heaven. We shall "see his face," and hear His voice, and speak with Him as friend with friend (Rev. 22:4). Sweet is the thought that whosoever may be wanting at the marriage supper, the Master Himself will be there. His presence will satisfy all our wants (Ps. 17:15).

What a sweet and glorious home heaven will be to those who have loved the Lord Jesus Christ in sincerity! Here we live by faith in Him, and find peace, though we see Him not. There we shall see Him face to face, and find He is altogether lovely. "Better" indeed will be the "sight of the eyes than the wandering of the desire" (Eccles. 6:9)!

But alas, how little fit for heaven are many who talk of "going to heaven" when they die, while they manifestly have no saving faith, and no real acquaintance with Christ. You give Christ no honor here. You have no communion with Him. You do not love Him. Alas! what could you do in heaven? It would be no place for you. Its joys would be no joys for you. Its happiness would be a happiness into which you could not enter. Its employ-ments would be a weariness and a burden to your heart. Oh, repent and change before it be too late!

I trust I have shown how deep are the foundations of that lit-tle expression, "Christ is all."

I might easily add to the things I have said, if space permit-ted. The subject is not exhausted. I have barely walked over the surface of it. There are mines of precious truth connected with it that I have left unopened.

I might show how *Christ ought to be all in a visible Church.* Splendid religious buildings, numerous religious services, gorgeous ceremonies, troops of ordained men, all, all are nothing in the sight of God, if the Lord Jesus Himself in all His offices is not honored, magnified, and exalted. That Church is but a dead carcass in which Christ is not "all."

I might show how *Christ ought to be all in a ministry.* The great work that ordained men are intended to do, is to lift up Christ. We are to be like the pole on which the brazen serpent was hung. We are useful so long as we exalt the great object of faith, but useful no further. We are to be ambassadors to carry tidings to a rebellious world about the King's Son, and if we teach men to think more about us and our office than about Him, we are not fit for our place. The Spirit will never honor that minister who does not testify of Christ—who does not make Christ "all."

I might show how language seems exhausted in the Bible, in describing Christ's various offices. I might describe how figures seem endless that are employed in unfolding Christ's fullness. The High Priest, the Mediator, the Redeemer, the Savior, the Advocate, the Shepherd, the Physician, the Bridegroom, the Head, the Bread of Life, the Light of the World, the Way, the Door, the Vine, the Rock, the Fountain, the Sun of Righteousness, the Forerunner, the Surety, the Captain, the Prince of Life, the Amen, the Almighty, the Author and Finisher of Faith, the Lamb of God, the King of Saints, the Wonderful, the Mighty God, the Counselor, the Bishop of Souls—all these, and many more, are names given to Christ in Scripture. Each is a fountain of instruction and comfort for everyone who is willing to drink of it. Each supplies matter for useful meditation.

But I trust I have said enough to throw light on the point I want to impress on the minds of all who read this chapter. I trust I have said enough to show the immense importance of the practical conclusions with which I now desire to finish the subject.

(a) Is Christ all? Then let us LEARN THE UTTER USELESSNESS OF A CHRIST-LESS RELIGION.

There are only too many baptized men and women who practically know nothing at all about Christ. Their religion consists in a few vague notions and empty expressions. "They trust they are no worse than others. They keep to their church. They try to do their duty. They do nobody any harm. They hope God will be merciful to them. They trust the Almighty will pardon their sins, and take them to heaven when they die." This is about the whole of their religion!

But what do these people know practically about Christ? Nothing: nothing at all! What experimental acquaintance have they with His offices and work, His blood, His righteousness, His mediation, His priesthood, His intercession? None: none at all! Ask them about a saving faith—ask them about being born again of the Spirit—ask them about being sanctified in Christ Jesus.

What answer will you get? You are a barbarian to them. You have asked them simple Bible questions. But they know no more about them experimentally than a Buddhist or a Turk. And yet this is the religion of hundreds and thousands of people who are called Christians, all over the world!

If any reader of this chapter is a man of this kind, I warn him plainly that such Christianity will never take him to heaven. It may do very well in the eye of man. It may pass muster very decently at the vestry-meeting, in the place of business, in the House of Commons, or in the streets. But it will never comfort you. It will never satisfy your conscience. It will never save your soul.

I warn you plainly that all notions and theories about God being merciful without Christ, and excepting through Christ, are baseless delusions and empty fancies. Such theories are as purely an idol of man's invention as the idol of Juggernaut. They are all of the earth, earthy. They never came down from heaven. The God of heaven has sealed and appointed Christ as the one only Savior and way of life, and all who would be saved must be content to be saved by Him, or they will never be saved at all.

Let every reader take notice. I give you fair warning this day. A religion without Christ will never save your soul.

(b) Let me say another thing. Is Christ all? Then LEARN THE ENORMOUS FOLLY OF JOINING ANYTHING WITH CHRIST IN THE MATTER OF SALVATION.

There are multitudes of baptized men and women who profess to honor Christ, but in reality do Him great dishonor. They give Christ a certain place in their system of religion, but not the place that God intended Him to fill. Christ alone is not "all in all" to their souls.—No! It is either Christ and the Church—or Christ and the sacraments—or Christ and His ordained ministers—or Christ and their own repentance—or Christ and their own goodness—or Christ and their own prayers—or Christ and their own sincerity and charity, on which they practically rest their souls.

If any reader of this chapter is a Christian of this kind, I warn him also plainly, that his religion is an offense to God. You are changing God's plan of salvation into a plan of your own devising. You are in effect deposing Christ from His throne, by giving the glory due to Him to another.

I care not who it is who teaches such religion and on whose word you build. Whether he be Pope or Cardinal, Archbishop or Bishop, Dean or Archdeacon, Presbyter or Deacon, Episcopalian or Presbyterian, Baptist or Independent, Wesleyan or Plymouth brother, whosoever adds anything to Christ teaches you wrong.

I care not what it is that you add to Christ. Whether it be the necessity of joining the Church of Rome, or of being an Episcopalian, or of becoming a Free Churchman, or of giving up the Liturgy, or of being dipped—whatever you may practically add to Christ in the matter of salvation, you do Christ an injury.

Take heed what you are doing. Beware of giving to Christ's servants the honor due to none but Christ. Beware of giving the

Lord's ordinances the honor due unto the Lord. Beware of resting the burden of your soul on anything but Christ, and Christ alone.

(c) Let me say another thing. Is Christ all? Then LET ALL WHO WANT TO BE SAVED, APPLY DIRECT TO CHRIST.

There are many who hear of Christ with the ear and believe all they are told about Him. They allow that there is no salvation excepting in Christ. They acknowledge that Jesus alone can deliver them from hell and present them faultless before God.

But they seem never to get beyond this general acknowledgment. They never fairly lay hold on Christ for their own souls. They stick fast in a state of wishing, and wanting, and feeling, and intending, and never get any further. They see what we mean: they know it is all true. They hope one day to get full benefit of it: but at present they get no benefit whatever. The world is their "all." Politics are their "all." Pleasure is their "all." Business is their "all." But Christ is not their all.

If any reader of this chapter is a man of this kind, I warn him also plainly, he is in a bad state of soul. You are as truly in the way to hell in your present condition, as Judas Iscariot, or Ahab, or Cain. Believe me, there must be actual faith in Christ, or else Christ died in vain so far as you are concerned. It is not looking at the bread that feeds the hungry man but the actual eating of it. It is not gazing on the lifeboat that saves the shipwrecked sailor, but actually getting into it. It is not knowing and believing that Christ is a Savior that can save your soul, unless there are actual transactions between you and Christ. You must be able to say,

"Christ is my Savior, because I have come to Him by faith, and taken Him for my own."—"Much of religion," said Luther, "turns on being able to use possessive pronouns. Take from me the word '*my*' and you take from me God!"

Hear the advice I give you this day, and act upon it at once. Stand still no longer, waiting for some imaginary frames and feelings, which will never come. Hesitate no longer under the idea that you must first of all obtain the Spirit and then come to Christ. Arise and come to Christ just as you are. He waits for you, and is as willing to save as He is mighty. He is the appointed Physician for sin-sick souls. Deal with Him as you would with your doctor about the cure of a disease of your body. Make a direct application to Him and tell Him all your wants. Take with you words this day, and cry mightily to the Lord Jesus for pardon and peace, as the thief did on the cross. Do as that man did: cry, "Lord, remember me" (Luke 23:42). Tell Him you have heard that He receives sinners, and that you are such. Tell Him you want to be saved and ask Him to save you. Rest not till you have actually tasted for yourself that the Lord is gracious. Do this and you shall find, sooner or later, if you are really in earnest, that "Christ is all."

(d) One more thing let me add. Is Christ all? Then LET ALL HIS CONVERTED PEOPLE DEAL WITH HIM AS IF THEY REALLY BELIEVED IT. LET THEM LEAN ON HIM AND TRUST HIM FAR MORE THAN THEY HAVE EVER DONE YET.

Alas, there are many of the Lord's people who live far below their privileges! There are many truly Christian souls who rob themselves of their own peace, and forsake their own mercies. There are many who insensibly join their own faith, or the work of the Spirit in their own hearts, to Christ, and so miss the fullness of Gospel peace. There are many who make little progress in their pursuit of holiness, and shine with a very dim light. And why is all this? Simply because in nineteen cases out of twenty men do not make Christ all in all.

Now I call on every reader of this chapter who is a believer, I beseech him for his own sake, to make sure that Christ is really and thoroughly his all in all. Beware of allowing yourself to mingle anything of your own with Christ.

Have you faith? It is a priceless blessing. Happy indeed are they who are willing and ready to trust Jesus. But take heed you do not make a Christ of your faith. Rest not on your own faith, but on Christ.

Is the work of the Spirit in your soul? Thank God for it. It is a work that shall never be overthrown. But oh, beware, lest, unaware to yourself, you make a Christ of the work of the Spirit! Rest not on the work of the Spirit, but on Christ.

Have you any inward feelings of religion and experience of grace? Thank God for it. Thousands have no more religious feeling than a cat or dog. But oh, beware lest you make a Christ of your feelings and sensations! They are poor, uncertain things and sadly dependent on our bodies and outward circumstances. Rest only on Christ.

Learn, I entreat you, to look more and more at the great *object of faith*, Jesus Christ, and to keep your mind dwelling on Him. So doing you would find faith, and all the other graces, grow, though the growth at the time might be imperceptible to yourself. He that would prove a skillful archer must not look at the arrow, but at the mark.

Alas, I fear there is a great piece of pride and unbelief still sticking in the hearts of many believers! Few seem to realize how much they need a Savior. Few seem to understand how thoroughly they are indebted to Him. Few seem to comprehend how much they need Him every day. Few seem to feel how simply and like a child they ought to hang their souls on Him. Few seem to be aware how full of love He is to His poor, weak people, and how ready to help them! And few therefore seem to know the peace, and joy, and strength, and power to live a godly life, which is to be had in Christ.

Change your plan, reader, if your conscience tells you you are guilty: change your plan, and learn to trust Christ more. Physicians love to see patients coming to consult them: it is their office to receive the sickly and, if possible, to effect cures. The advocate loves to be employed: it is his calling. The husband loves his wife to trust him and lean upon him: it is his delight to cherish her and promote her comfort. And Christ loves His people to lean on Him, to rest in Him, to call on Him, to abide in Him.

Let us all learn and strive to do so more and more. Let us live on Christ. Let us live in Christ. Let us live with Christ. Let us live to Christ. So doing, we shall prove that we fully realize that "Christ is all." So doing, we shall feel great peace, and attain more of that "holiness without which no man shall see the Lord" (Heb. 12:14).

1. Number 20 in the complete book.

BRINGING YOU THE TIMELESS CLASSICS

Classics

... these are key books that every believer on the journey of spiritual formation should read.

Power Through Prayer
ISBN-13: 978-0-8024-5662-5

The Christian's Secret of a Happy Life
ISBN-13: 978-0-8024-5656-4

Hudson Taylor's Spiritual Secret
ISBN-13: 978-0-8024-5658-8

The Incomparable Christ
ISBN-13: 978-0-8024-5660-1

Orthodoxy
ISBN-13: 978-0-8024-5657-1

The Apostolic Fathers
ISBN-13: 978-0-8024-5659-5

MOODY
Publishers

From the Word to Life

moodypublishers.com

BRINGING YOU THE TIMELESS CLASSICS

Classics